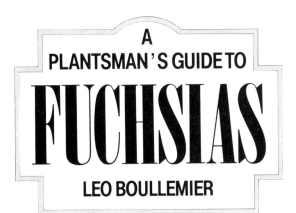

A
PLANTSMAN'S GUIDE TO
FUCHSIAS

LEO BOULLEMIER

A
PLANTSMAN'S GUIDE TO
FUCHSIAS

LEO BOULLEMIER

SERIES EDITOR
ALAN TOOGOOD

WARD LOCK LIMITED · LONDON

Text © Ward Lock Ltd 1989
Line drawings © Ward Lock Ltd 1989

First published in Great Britain in 1989
by Ward Lock Limited, 8 Clifford Street
London W1X 1RB, an Egmont Company

House editor Denis Ingram

Text film in Times Roman
by Dorchester Typesetting
Printed and bound in Great Britain by
Hazell Watson & Viney Ltd,
Member of the BPCC Group,
Aylesbury, Bucks.

British Library Cataloguing in Publication Data

Boullemier, Leo B.
    A plantsman's guide to fuchsias
    1.   Gardens. Fuchsias. Cultivation
    I.   Title   II. Series
    635.9′3344

ISBN 0-7063-6738-3

CONTENTS

PUBLISHER'S NOTE

Readers are requested to note that in order to make the text intelligible in both hemispheres, plant flowering times, etc. are described in terms of seasons, not months. The following table provides an approximate 'translation' of seasons into months for the two hemispheres.

Northern Hemisphere		Southern Hemisphere
Mid-winter	= January	= Mid-summer
Late winter	= February	= Late summer
Early spring	= March	= Early autumn
Mid-spring	= April	= Mid-autumn
Late spring	= May	= Late autumn
Early summer	= June	= Early winter
Mid-summer	= July	= Mid-winter
Late summer	= August	= Late winter
Early autumn	= September	= Early spring
Mid-autumn	= October	= Mid-spring
Late autumn	= November	= Late spring
Early winter	= December	= Early summer

Captions for colour photographs on chapter opening pages:

Pp. 8-9 A magnificent fuchsia border in high summer. This rich display is built from bush and standard plants.
Pp. 20-21 The American cultivar 'Roy Walker' is probably the best of the very few upright-growing double whites.
Pp. 40-41 'Red Spider' takes its name from its rich rose corolla, pendant sepals and long pedicels.
Pp. 68-69 A recent variety and a challenge to the grower, 'Mickey Goult' bears smallish flowers but is always in bloom.
Pp. 100-101 'Sapphire' is an outstanding cultivar which holds its colour better than most of the blues.
Pp. 112-113 'Walsingham', a beautiful pastel-shaded cultivar, even outshines its lovely parent 'Blush o' Dawn'.
Pp. 120-121 'Pride of the West' is a vigorous grower only suitable as a climber.

EDITOR'S FOREWORD

This unique series takes a completely fresh look at the most popular garden and greenhouse plants.

Written by a team of leading specialists, yet suitable for novice and more experienced gardener alike, the series considers modern uses of the plants, including refreshing ideas for combining them with other garden or greenhouse plants. This should appeal to the more general gardener who, unlike the specialist, does not want to devote a large part of the garden to a particular plant. Many of the planting schemes and modern uses are beautifully illustrated in colour.

The extensive A-Z lists describe in great detail hundreds of the best varieties and species available today.

For the historically-minded, each book opens with a brief history of the subject up to the present day and, as appropriate, looks at the developments by plant breeders.

The books cover all you need to know about growing and propagating. The former embraces such aspects as suitable sites and soils, planting methods, all-year-round care and how to combat pests, diseases and disorders.

Propagation includes raising plants from seeds and by vegetative means, as appropriate.

For each subject there is a society (sometimes more), full of details which round-off each book.

The plants that make up this series are very popular and examples can be found in many gardens. However, it is hoped that these books will encourage gardeners to try some of the better, or perhaps more unusual, varieties; ensure some stunning plant associations; and result in the plants being grown well.

Alan Toogood

CHAPTER ONE

PAST AND PRESENT

The fuchsia is not an old-fashioned English plant and, being an interloper – mainly from South America – has to be grown in the correct environment. To grow and flower to full potential cultivation should imitate the natural conditions of the species, which grow in the wild on high mountain slopes with heavy rainfall. The fuchsia is not, as many people imagine, a house plant, where the dry atmosphere is totally unsuitable, but it flourishes in the summer bed or border or, best of all, in a protected area in the open. Being often sub-tropical in origin, its main requirements are moderate warmth, moisture, shade, humidity and, if under glass, plenty of ventilation.

Grown either as half-hardies or hardy cultivars fuchsias are the most rewarding for a continuous summer display. Not only do they flower freely but the number of cultivars which can be purchased more cheaply than most other plants run into many thousands and can be trained into numerous recognized forms and shapes. Fuchsias need few special skills, are easy to cultivate (any reasonably fertile soil will suit their requirements) and, given those moist conditions and adequate light, will flourish to near perfection, laden with exotic, delicate and graceful blooms.

EARLY HISTORY
AND
DEVELOPMENT

The very first mention of the fuchsia is in the fourteenth century, when it is known that the Incas in Peru were cultivating the species *F. boliviana* for edible berries. The fuchsia, like many things, was found accidentally when the Old World was expanding in the late seventeenth century to newly discovered lands. Their progress was hampered by the scourge of malaria, with eminent botanists of the day being commissioned to locate sources of the cinchona tree, from which quinine was extracted.

One such botanist was Father Carole Plumier (1646–1704), a Minin monk, searching in the foothills of Santo Domingo on the island of Hispaniola. (Later research suggests the actual location is more likely to have been Haiti on the same island.) It was here, some time between 1689 and 1697, that Plumier came across his greatest find, an unusual, shrubby plant with scarlet flowers and coppery bronze foilage, *Fuchsia triphylla flore coccinea*. In 1703 Plumier inaccurately described and illustrated his find in *Nova Plantarum Americanum Genera* in Paris and dedicated it to Dr Leonhart Fuchs, the sixteenth-century doctor of medicine and herbalist. *Fuchsia triphylla* was then lost to the fuchsia world until 1873.

In 1725 R.P.L. Feuillée, a pupil of Plumier, published an accurate drawing of the Chilean *F.magellanica*, under the native name of Thilco. Philip Miller, in *Miller's Dictionary of Gardening* in 1739, reports having *F. triphylla* in cultivation at Chelsea Physic Garden from seeds sent by Dr William Houstoun before 1733. This, however, lacks confirmation of what would have been the first introduction of the fuchsia into Europe. In 1757 Linnaeus classified the genus *Fuchsia* from Plumier's inaccurate drawing as a species in the *Tetrandria Monogynis* in the first edition of *Species Plantarum*. From 1787 the introduction of several species was fairly frequent, the first to be mentioned being *F. arborescens*, collected by Martín Sessé in Mexico.

Just how the first plant arrived in England will always be subject to conjecture, but it would appear that a Captain Firth in 1788, after his return from South America, sent to Kew what he called *F. coccinea*. There is some doubt whether this was actually *F. coccinea* from Brazil or *F. magellanica*

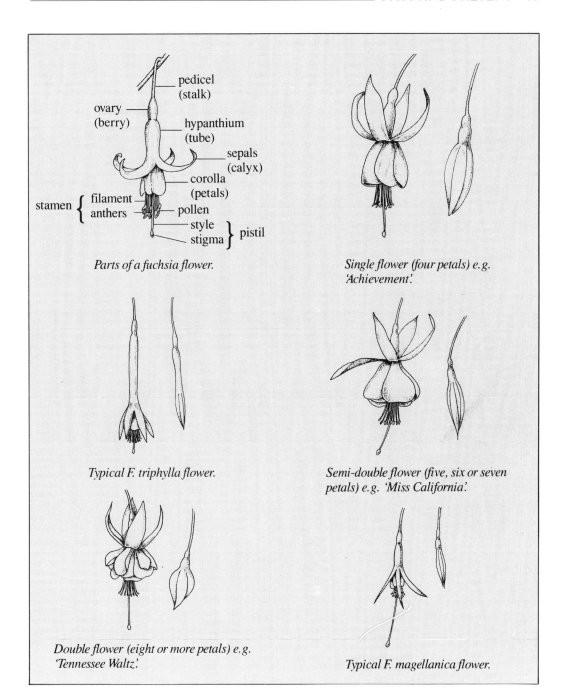

Parts of a fuchsia flower.

pedicel (stalk)
ovary (berry)
hypanthium (tube)
sepals (calyx)
corolla (petals)
stamen { filament, anthers }
pollen
style
stigma } pistil

Single flower (four petals) e.g. 'Achievement'.

Typical F. triphylla flower.

Semi-double flower (five, six or seven petals) e.g. 'Miss California'.

Double flower (eight or more petals) e.g. 'Tennessee Waltz'.

Typical F. magellanica flower.

Fuchsia perscandens from New Zealand – considerably different from our usual idea of a fuchsia.

Fuchsia fulgens var. rubra grandiflora, one of the most beautiful of the species, is easy to grow. It makes tuberous roots.

from Chile; both are extremely similar and proved to be hardy.

It was around this time that the same species was being offered for sale by the Hammersmith nurseryman James Lee at his Vineyard Nursery, where the present Olympia Halls now stand. Another species, *F. lycioides*, with tiny pink flowers from the Atacama desert is reported growing at Hampton Court in 1796 and also in the King's Garden at Kew. *F. arborescens* was introduced into Europe by Bullock in 1823 from seeds obtained in Mexico, resulting in the first recording of the crossing of *F. coccinea* and *F. macrostemma* with *F. arborescens* in 1825. In the same year *F. excorticata* was raised from seed collected in New Zealand by Richardson, at Colville's nursery in England. By 1827 *F. microphylla* and *F. thymifolia* had been introduced into England, and these, with *F. arborescens*, were being grown in the conservatories and winter gardens owned by the wealthy.

THE HYBRIDIZERS

It was during the 1820s and 1830s that the growers and nurserymen of the day turned their attention to hybridizing and it was due to the skill and patience of these breeders that we were rewarded with the first recorded hybrid when Bunney of Stratford, London, crossed either *F. coccinea* or *F. conica* with *F. microphylla* to obtain in 1832 'Globosa', a hybrid with a very short tube.

A few years later *F. fulgens* from Mexico was introduced by Theodor Hartweg. *F. fulgens* was totally different from any other species in circulation at that time, having a very long orange-red tube with short sepals and petals with very large foliage. This was to have an influence upon later cultivars: both W. Chandler in 1839 and Standish of Bagshot in 1840 used *F. fulgens* crossed with forms of *F. magellanica* to give their first hybrids of 'Chandlerii' and 'Standishii'. By 1840 several nurserymen were hybridizing and these included Epps of Maidstone, Harrison of Dereham and May. Illustrations and pictures of Standish crossings appeared in the *Botanical Register* for 1842 and included his earliest raisings: 'Aurora', 'Attraction' ('Attractor'), 'Colossus' and the well-known cultivar still grown today, 'President'.

Up to 1840 the only colours in hybrids being produced were red and purple or red and blue, the reds having several different shades, but the breakthrough came in that year with 'Venus Victrix', a very weak grower with small flowers. 'Venus Victrix' occurred in the garden of Mr Gulliver in Herstmonceux, as a chance seedling from *F. magellanica*. It was the first fuchsia with white tube and sepals and is used extensively for hybridizing, even to this day.

The first list of fuchsias appears in 1844 when Félix M. Porcher in France listed some 300 species and varieties in his first edition of *Le Fuchsia, son Histoire et sa Culture*, followed in 1848 by his second edition, this time with 520 species and varieties.

In 1848 William Storey of Newton Abbot produced the first striped corolla, a single striped pink and blue named 'Striata'. His first released seedling, also in 1848, was 'Elegantissima', a scarlet and deep purple. These were followed by the first doubles in 1850 with 'Duplex', a semi-double of crimson and purple, and 'Multiplex', a true double resembling a double violet. Storey then produced in 1854 the first fuchsias with white petals, the sister seedlings 'Mrs Storey' and 'Queen Victoria'. Yet another breakthrough came in 1852 when Mr Dominy at Veitch's nursery crossed *F. denticulata* with *F. macrostigma* to produce the winter-flowering 'Dominyana'.

By now the French raisers were hybridizing; Victor Lemoine's famous nursery in Nancy, during its existence produced between 300 and 400 cultivars and Cornelissen in Belgium was also hybridizing around 1857. It was during the 1850s and the 1860s that many British hybridizers names appear, such as Banks, Bull, Cripps, Henderson, Miller, Youell to name but a few, producing such cultivars as 'Black Prince' 'Brilliant', 'Mauve Beauty', 'Lustre', 'Rose of Castile', 'Rose of Denmark', 'Corallina' and 'Pontey's Tricolour', which still hold their own among the cultivars of today.

Fuchsia history cannot be complete without mentioning the name of James Lye of Trowbridge, who started hybridizing in 1860 and by 1889 had produced 82 cultivars including such famous names as 'Amy Lye', 'Charming', 'Duchess of Albany', 'James Lye' and 'Lye's Unique', all having the 'Lye hallmark' of a beautiful, solid, rich creamy white tube and waxlike sepals. Not only a great hybridizer, he was

described as the Champion Fuchsia Grower with his exhibition pillars and pyramids, 2.5–3 m (8–10 ft) high and over a metre (4 ft) through the base.

As previously mentioned, the original *F. triphylla* disappeared after it had been discovered by Plumier and did not reappear for almost 180 years, until Thomas Hogg rediscovered it by collecting seed in Haiti (Hispaniola) to send home to America. Subsequently grown plants from this seed were received in Britain from New York by Henderson's nursery of St John's Wood, London, the site on which MCC Lords Cricket Ground now stands. They were identified by Kew Botanical Gardens in 1882. Assuming this information is correct, and there seems no reason to doubt its authenticity, the white-tubed hybrid called 'Thalia' attributed to Turner, the nurseryman at Slough in 1855, could not have been a *triphylla* cross, as it was originally described, but a cultivar raised from 'Venus Victrix' and recorded in the *Gardener's Chronicle* of 1875.

This period was the heyday of the fuchsia. The Victorians adored their fuchsias, almost every household of note had its collection, gardening magazines of the day were full of culture hints on their care, and between 30 and 40 new introductions were being raised each year.

Another development took place in 1901, this time in the shape of the flower. H. Cannell of Swanley produced 'Swanley Gem', a rich scarlet and violet single, but with four flawless petals, opening flat to make a perfect circle.

Neue Fuchsien:

1. *Schwan.*   4. *Goliath.*
2. *Majestica*   5. *Erinnerung an Humboldt.*
3. *Spectabilis.*   6. *Fürst A. Schwarzenberg.*
7. *Fürstin v. Dietrichstein.*

(Above) *'New introductions' from about 1850 as portrayed on an old German print.*

(Opposite) *'Venus Victrix', a mutant found in 1840, was the very first fuchsia with white tube and sepals. Difficult to grow.*

THE FIRST SOCIETIES

From 1890 the popularity of the fuchsia began to decline and by the outbreak of the First World War, it was almost lost, except for private collections and the few left in the hands of some nurserymen. After the war, everyone rebelled against anything Victorian and the fuchsia fell into complete disfavour, the new craze under glass being tomatoes.

A few raisers were at work in California, however, and in 1929 the American Fuchsia Society was founded, followed by the Fuchsia Society in Britain in 1938. After the Second World War two notable things occurred in the United States. A few American raisers, including Greene and Hazard, saw the potential of the fuchsia and in 1930 the American Fuchsia Society sent three of their officers to England, seeking cultivars from which they could start a hybridizing programme in California. With the assistance of the Royal Horticultural Society, they collected 51 desirable cultivars, 48 of which survived the long journey, and George Budgen of Berkeley Horticultural Nursery was selected to propagate and introduce them to Californian growers.

Among these cultivars were 'Rolla', 'Aurora Superba', 'The Doctor', 'Lustre Improved', 'Mrs W. Rundle', 'Pink Pearl', 'Rose of Denmark' and 'Countess of Aberdeen'. It was through these efforts that great strides were made in the field of American hybridizing and among those who deserve the credit were Victor Reiter, Gustave Niederholzer, Horce Tiret, Hugh Hazard and

Bessie Hazard. Nearly all the vast number of new cultivars to be exported from America for the next 30 to 40 years were descendants from these original plants. One notable new introduction was the first 'all white', 'Flying Cloud' by Reiter.

Another landmark of fuchsia history was the publication in 1936 of the *Check List of Fuchsias* by Dr E. O. Essig, listing almost 2000 cultivars and species, which was considered at the time an authoritative work. The Americans took up the challenge of hybridizing in a big way and were quickly producing new cultivars which seemed to be produced on the conveyor belt system; 20, then 30, then 40 each year, rising fast to 213 in 1987 and 129 in 1988. It must be said, however, that in the latter years these figures are the number of new introductions registered with the American Fuchsia Society; the actual number of American introductions now being relatively small. The reason for this great expansion early on was the fact that hybridizing in America was performed by professional growers, whereas in Britain, apart from very few exceptions, all hybridizing was carried out by amateurs. In 1943 Dr Philip Munz published *A Revision of the Genus Fuchsia (Onagraceae)* which classified some 100 species, the authoritative work for many years until subsequent taxonomists, particularly Dr Paul Berry in the USA, carried out further revision work.

It was in the 1960s that the British hybridizers made great inroads, first with Alfred Thornley of Preston (Preston Guild and Ravensbarrow) and Dr

O. Colville in Bath, followed by Cliff Gadsby who worked upon erect-flowering cultivars with 'Upward Look' and 'Cloverdales'; his cultivar 'Lady Isobel Barnett' probably being the most floriferous ever. Bob Pacey at Melton Mowbray took up his work when Gadsby died and is still producing fine introductions. In America during the 1960s Ted Paskesen, Michael Pennisi and Roy Walker were all producing outstanding new introductions which were soon grown extensively in Britain too. In 1968 two chance seedlings were to become quite famous: 'La Campanella' by John Blackwell of Swindon and 'Mieke Meursing' found by Fred Hopgood under a plant of 'RAF' on his staging in Surrey, both varieties being outstanding on account of their floriferousness and exhibition potential.

The 1970s were vintage years for British hybridizers, firstly with Dr Matthew Ryle producing, among many, 'Annabel', 'Border Queen' and 'Lady Kathleen Spence', the only cultivar to receive a BFS Gold Award. George Roe produced a long list of outstanding introductions, mainly from 'Lustre', to give us 'Micky Goult', 'Alison Ewart' and 'Nellie Nuttall'. John Wright of Reading was interbreeding with the species to produce the 'Whiteknight'

and 'Lechlade' series of introductions.

Dave Clark of Merseyside also entered the hybridizing field, while in the Netherlands Herman de Graaf commenced his new breeding programme, using species not previously exploited, particularly *F. lycioides* and *F. magdalenae*. Eddie Goulding was also beginning his extensive range of new cultivars, which included the first white *triphylla*, 'Our Ted'.

The 1980s have produced other new raisers in Len Bielby of Hull, Fred Redfern of Derby and Eric Johns of Harrogate, all of whom are working with new material, while in New Zealand Bob Sharpe of Wellington has produced a range of new exciting cultivars. We have now reached the stage, with between 8000 and 10,000 recorded fuchsias, where our hybridizers must be much more selective in their breeding material to ensure future introductions are an improvement upon existing ones. With this huge number of fuchsias, demand has grown in recent years for a comprehensive check list. Little was achieved, possibly due to the sheer size and magnitude of the task, until I produced the *Fuchsia Check List* of almost 8000 species, hybrids and cultivars, now accepted by all societies and enthusiasts throughout the world.

CHAPTER TWO

PLANTING IDEAS

One of my conclusions concerning the cultivation of fuchsias, after many years' experience, is that they grow better and are more prolific with bloom when grown outside than when cultivated under the protection of glass. Our greenhouses should be almost empty from midsummer until housing again in mid-autumn for overwintering. During this period, with high temperatures under glass, our fuchsias almost refuse to grow.

Remember most species originate in South America, so their natural habitat is at a high altitude in moisture-laden cloud; dappled shade through the evergreen forests, with the mean temperature of 13°C (55°F) and high rainfall.

That is the environment we should try to imitate, and we will succeed better outside. For protection from the elements' excesses, shade houses or tunnels constructed of plastic woven netting provide real enthusiasts with the ideal environment: shade from heat and burning sun and shelter from strong winds, yet at the same time affording complete ventilation and allowing natural rainfall to penetrate. Even our top showmen are employing this method, by using their greenhouses only to flower their plants, bringing them in two or three weeks before their shows.

After the early aspects of cultivation – pruning, repotting, potting-on and stopping – plants should be outside in the border, on the patio, under pergolas, or in formal schemes by early summer. They will need a sheltered position, thriving in shade and with moisture; on the other hand, they are not bog plants or shade-loving plants. Filtered sun is ideal, the *triphyllas* and a few others will take full sun, but all definitely need protection from excessive, hot, drying winds.

Given these conditions, plants grown outside are more floriferous, tougher and less prone to pests and diseases, even lax-growing cultivars (those between upright and trailing) become stiff uprights. Flowering can begin in early summer, reaching its peak during the late summer and autumn until the first frosts (just watch for the change in growth and flower as soon as the early morning and overnight dews appear); we have that wonderful mass display few other plants can match.

Which are the ways to grow fuchsia outdoors?

> (a) in pots or containers for patio, terrace or garden decoration,
> (b) as half-hardies in the garden or border,
> (c) hardy plants as permanent shrubs.

FUCHSIAS IN CONTAINERS

The best plants are two-, three- or four-year-old plants which have received the protection of frost-free conditions, been pruned and repotted, then potted on again into their final containers. The time to place them outside, particularly on the patio or terrace will depend upon weather conditions, usually after hardening off in early summer in a semi-shaded position. They should never lack moisture and a constant watch must be maintained, as plants in any container dry out so very quickly. Feeding and staking will also have to be maintained, but once in their final position, plants will not require any further stopping.

□ TUBS

A display of planted tubs can enhance any garden, pathway or patio and they now come in a large variety of sizes and materials. The best are those made in wood, stone, concrete and terracotta, but there are attractive plastic planters available. Plastic tubs are usually the cheapest, but be selective as thin ones quickly become brittle, either by exposure to the sun or from frost. Plastic tubs do not insulate well against the frost and should never be left outside during the winter. Terracotta pots and urns look attractive, but make sure they are frost proof as otherwise a few degrees of frost will crack them.

In all cases tubs must have adequate drainage holes to allow surplus water to drain away. Without sufficient drainage, tubs will slowly fill with water, especially during the winter months, causing the roots to rot or become frozen. A 45 cm (18 in) pot should have three drainage holes and a 60 cm (24 in) one four drainage holes. Plants grown in tubs, or any container, are at the mercy of their owner and should never want for moisture. During dry periods tubs need watering every day, and even during drizzle or light rain they still require water. Feeding should be programmed with a liquid fertilizer from mid-spring to the finish of flowering in mid-autumn.

Soil from the garden is not good enough for growing plants in tubs. Soilless composts are excellent but do dry out quickly and so need more attention than those which contain a proportion of loam. The ideal compost would be a soilless compost incorporating 20% loam. (This may be difficult to locate, although Humber Manures of Stoneferry, Hull, do market such a mixture.)

Tubs are ideal containers for the patio or the terrace, adding that extra dimension and taking away bareness. And fuchsias are admirable subjects for tubs, whether planted separately or with

other plants. Standards are a very good choice, either half-standards, those with a stem of between 45 and 75 cm long (18–30 in), or full standards, with stems up to 105 cm (42 in).

The best cultivars for standards include: 'Barbara', 'Celia Smedley', 'Display', 'Hidcote Beauty', Lye's cultivars (any), 'Other Fellow' and 'Snowcap'. If the tub is large enough a variety of flowers could be planted around the base of the standard. Those that excel, with continuous flowering, include ageratum, semperflorens begonias, celosias, heliotropes, impatiens, lobelia, marigolds, verbenas and petunias (the F1 Express series do exceptionally well). With fuchsia standards in tubs it is imperative that adequate staking is provided as strong winds can snap a head off completely, destroying in seconds all the cultivation of months and even years.

Should you consider the bush or shrub type of fuchsia for your tubs, then try the tall, vigorous cultivars such as 'Display', 'Celia Smedley' or 'Snowcap'.

□ WINDOW BOXES

Window boxes are not exploited as fully as they should be. A desirable position would be on the side of the house receiving the morning sun; exposed to full sun all day, fuchsias resent the heat and plants will soon dry out. To obtain the best results fuchsias should be planted by themselves rather than with a mixture of different kinds of plants. If you do mix, then obvious choices would include zonal geraniums, begonias, celosias, marigolds and salvias. When

(Opposite) *A bold show from a container filled with the suitably-named 'Display'.* (Above) *A display of the single-flowered 'Coachman' at the Dutch National Show.*

selecting fuchsias avoid the very stiff, upright growers; the best type would be of lax habit such as 'Carmen Marie', 'Lena', 'Jack Shahan', 'Mrs Marshall', 'Molesworth' and 'Swingtime'. Window boxes require fresh soil with new plants each season, as plants in their very exposed position during the summer rarely overwinter satisfactorily. Planting should be done in early summer, with plants properly hardened off. Firm them into place well with your fingers, but do not use anything to ram the soil down. Plants must never want for water and apart from copious watering, will appreciate spraying, either before the sun has gained its power, or in the early evening. A balanced feeding programme is particularly important (see pp. 76–81).

□ 'PORTABLE GARDENS'

The growing of large specimen fuchsias in the form of pillars, conicals and espaliers as permanent subjects outside

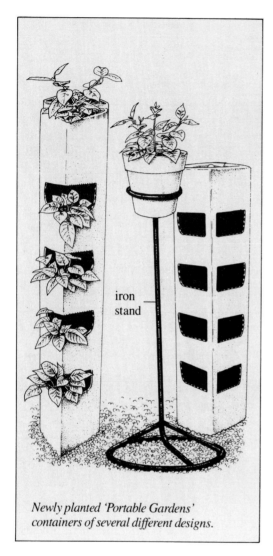

iron
stand

*Newly planted 'Portable Gardens'
containers of several different designs.*

ten fuchsias in one unit, obtaining the effect of a huge shrub within twelve weeks of planting. Most effective is the use of a single cultivar, preferably one with a bushy or slightly lax growth, such as 'Border Queen', 'Lena' or 'Snowcap'. You can even create an instant pillar by stacking two or even three units on top of each other.

□ PERGOLAS

Pergolas in the garden add a third dimension, by adding vertical interest in shape and form, leaving plenty of scope for skill and artistic flair. Arches and pergolas made of wood look superb, their shape can be used to advantage when built to suit the garden, and harsh lines can be softened with suitable plantings.

Constructed over a patio area a pergola reinforces the idea of an outside room. Trellis panels can be fixed to provide extra shelter, and the closely spaced roof beams covered with climbing plants offer protection from the sun and create conditions supremely suited to fuchsias. The focal point of a free-standing pergola, if a statue or bird bath is not used, could be a large tub housing a specimen shrub or full standard fuchsia. Suitable cultivars could include 'Celia Smedley', 'Display', 'Mrs Lovell Swisher' or 'Snowcap', once they are at least two years old.

Hanging baskets would be an automatic choice for suspending from the cross beams, filled, perhaps, with fuchsias such as 'Harry Gray', 'Jack Shahan', 'La Campanella', 'Marinka' or 'Walsingham'.

is usually extremely difficult and hardly feasible for most gardeners. Such specimens take up to five years of training to full flowering stage and are difficult to overwinter successfully. But, by using free-standing units not unlike tubs for strawberry-growing, you can plant up to

BEDS and BORDERS

Even with the vagaries of our climate it is still not difficult to provide conditions similar to the natural habitat of the fuchsia; and as long as growing conditions afford cool roots together with some shade for top growth, what better place for them than our garden beds and borders? The fuchsia is so versatile it can be considered for many traditional formal planting schemes, most popular being the half-hardies bedded out with other flowering and foliage plants, but fuchsias look good even in sub-tropical schemes, with such plants as cannas and ricinus.

Certain colours perform better than others when bedded out; red and purple flowers will thrive anywhere, as will the 'red and whites'. Sun lovers include the orange-coloured flowers in which class the *triphyllas* fall. White flowers and the 'pink and whites' are the most demanding; all prefer shade and if exposed to permanent sun, whites become pink bordering on rosy red. Trailing fuchsias are of course useless planted in beds, and in any case very few are hardy. Variegated and ornamental foliage fuchsias are well suited for bedding schemes, flourishing upon a lot of light but as little moisture as possible; 'Cloth of Gold' and 'Tom West' make good bushes but are frost-shy, *F. magellanica* var. *gracilis variegata* and 'Genii' are both attractive and hardy.

The planting of fuchsias as bedders is very convenient as they should go out in early summer, coinciding exactly with the summer bedding plants. Plants will have spent their previous few months in the congenial conditions of the greenhouse and should be reasonably hardened off before planting. They would be ideal if not in flower, but just coming into bud and growing in at least 12 cm (5 in) pots; anything smaller will be passing its time making growth and roots and not flowering until later in the season.

The ground or the border should have been well prepared, be well drained and have plenty of peat worked in, together with an application of a 1–1–1 ratio fertilizer such as Growmore. Planting can take place any time after the last frost.

We have a choice of two methods:

> (a) planting directly into the ground,
> (b) planting in the ground in pots.

The first approach produces the best display, will reduce the watering, and will enable plants to produce a better root system, but it will mean autumn lifting and potting up again in containers. To compensate for this, there will be a better and longer flowering period; and should autumn cuttings be required, far superior and more numerous shoots will be produced.

Planting fuchsias out in their pots is easier, flowering will be earlier, due to restricted roots and, come the autumn, plants can be lifted complete in their pots without disturbing their roots. The disadvantage is that even those pots plunged in the ground to their rims dry out quickly. During moderate weather conditions the hosepipe is possibly the

(Opposite, above) *A summer show of fuchsias in a garden in Canterbury, Kent.*
(Opposite, below) *'Celia Smedley' is an ideal cultivar for planting in containers on a patio. This is a 3-year-old plant.*
(Above) *'Schiller', the oldest fuchsia in the world, planted in 1899 and still growing in Ventura, California.*

best method of keeping the plants moist.

A regular feeding programme should be carried out, while the planting depth, whether in pots or not, should be fairly deep. As all fuchsias are very shallow rooters, routine hoeing and forking over should be carried out with care – hand weeding is the solution. When selecting the site, try if possible to choose one with semi-shade; sun in the morning and shade in the afternoon or *vice-versa*; the

hot mid-day sun is very demanding on fuchsias, as is hot, drying wind.

☐ BEDDING SCHEMES
An ideal scheme would incorporate half- and full standards securely staked, dotted liberally among ground cover of the best bedding annuals. Height is all important, especially where plants are central in beds or at the rear of borders. A brilliant display can be obtained using 'Bon Accorde', 'Celia Smedley', 'Barbara' and 'Snowcap' as standards, with the Organdy series of semperflorens begonias interspersed with *Cineraria maritima* 'Silver Dust'. Another equally good bedding plant is the new F_1 Accent impatiens which can be used to excellent effect with heliotrope 'Marine'. The F_1 ageratum interplanted with

alyssum is also very effective. Lobelia 'Crystal Palace' blends well with the Organdy begonias, while F₁ marigolds, either French or African, are extremely weather-tolerant. Fiery red salvias add that touch of vivid display, while verbenas are early flowering, with pretty shades of most colours. For edging, use alternanthera, the highly coloured foliage plant which grows only 23 cm (9 in) high. Further flowering plants include the various tuberous begonias and the red and yellow Cockscomb and Plumosa celosias. Kochia can be used as dot plants, making neat, light green clumps 60 cm (24 in) high which turn red in the autumn, giving them their common name of burning bushes. White and crimson nicotiana (tobacco plants) 60–90cm (2–3 ft) grow well even in shade, while pink, red and white geraniums (average height 45 cm, 18 in) stand both sun and shade. With the bush or shrub fuchsias used in bedding schemes, besides adding colour with annuals, we can add the 60 cm (24 in) high yellow potentilla, together with foliage plants such as the lily-like hosta, which thrives in shady places, and the Australian silk oak (*Grevillea robusta*).

☐ MASS PLANTING

When considering mass planting with dwarf fuchsias in bedding schemes or as ground cover, two series are particularly useful: the Thumb family ('Tom Thumb', 'Lady Thumb' and 'Son of Thumb') which grow no higher than 30cm (12in) and the Seven Dwarfs: 'Happy', 'Doc', 'Sleepy', 'Sneezy', 'Bashful', 'Grumpy' and 'Dopy' are only

23–37cm (9–15in) in height. All are hardy. Ageratums of the Adriatic strain would act as a wonderful ground foil, being only 10cm (4in) high.

☐ COLOUR CONTRAST

The preparation of bedding schemes involves some knowledge of those combinations of colours and hues which enhance each other. Since all plants will have leaves the one colour which may not be avoided is green. To produce harmonies which take this foliage green into consideration, it is necessary to use that portion of the spectrum which includes the yellows, the range of apricots and orange colours and the reds of vermilion hue. It is as well to avoid certain discordant effects, such as combining scarlet and crimson or orange and the well-named 'shocking pink'. Blues and mauves are unhappy together and so are magentas and purples. Brilliant effects can be obtained by using complementary colours – a mass of blue set off by some orange; yellow finds its complement in purple, whilst the reds are taken care of by the predominant green of foliage. When beds are planned, white, yellow and other pale colours look well in the foreground, with mauves and blues (separated) predominating in the background.

☐ SUB-TROPICAL SCHEMES

Both fuchsia standards and bush or shrub plants are perfectly acceptable when associated with sub-tropical bedding schemes. These could include as dot plants the yellow and red canna lilies which grow to 60 or 90cm (2–3ft).

Datura, with its striking flowers, could be used as a focal centrepiece, but requires a good deal of room, as does the lovely green and bronze foliage dot plant, ricinus, with leaves 90–150cm (3–5ft) high. *Cordyline australis* is another exotic-looking plant with grassy rush-like leaves, as is *Eucalyptus citriodora*, carrying fragrant lemon-scented leaves. Both are fine foliage plants.

HARDY SHRUBS

Hardies can be used as permanent shrubs, flowering either in beds or in borders, on the rockery or used as screens or hedges. One word of caution: no tall plants such as standards or conicals should be considered as permanent subjects and left out for the winter. This is also applicable to hardies grown in containers and left on the patio – all upward growth above soil level will be taken by frost as the walls of the containers will not protect them at all from freezing air.

What therefore is an adequate definition of a hardy fuchsia?

'Plant sending out new growth from the basal caul every spring. Able to resist late frost and if seared by frost, continue to grow away from the searing without stunting. Would be self-branching, bear good flowers from midsummer until bad light or autumn frosts. Needing no other protection other than the dead fronds and could be classified as a woody perennial.' – *British Fuchsia Soc.*

The range of hardy cultivars is now considerably greater than most growers realize – the days have passed when all were red and purple. We now have most colours, including pinks, whites and even delicate pastel shades. There are over 200 different hardy cultivars now available from specialist nurseries.

Preparation for the site is the same as for the half-hardies: good drainage with plenty of peat. As the height varies very considerably, from 20cm (8in) to 1.2–1.8m (4–6ft), it is imperative when planting that the ultimate height of growth is known to prevent having tall plants at the front and dwarf plants at the back of borders.

Another important aspect is the actual planting time, which is early summer. This will enable plants to become established before the autumn. Do not plant out in late summer or autumn as this will leave no time for the plant to establish itself and it will possibly be lost. Another pitfall to watch is the planting out of plants too small – it is utterly useless to plant out anything from a pot less than 10cm (4in). When planting, the depth should be several inches deeper than normal; this is to protect the crown and roots from frost during the winter and to assist in producing early basal shoots the following spring. A good method is to hollow out a shallow hole some 8 or 10cm (3 or 4in) deep and 20 or 25cm (8 or 10in) in diameter. In the centre have a hole to receive the rootball, firming in well with heavy finger pressure. Subsequently, the summer rain and watering will bring the soil around the plant to its normal height, leaving the base well below the soil.

At no time during the summer must

This huge container-grown plant at Wallington Hall, Northumberland, is an unidentified Lye's cultivar of great age.

'Border Queen' seen in full flower a mere eight weeks after it was planted.

the new plant lack moisture; water frequently to help it to become established and, if possible, spray overhead in the evening.

Let the hardies finish their flowering naturally, do not prune in the autumn, although taking down by one-third will do no harm. The growth left will act as a certain amount of protection against the frosts. Should the winter be severe, the crown of hardies could be covered (although this is not really necessary) with some protection such as peat, sand or old potting compost – leaves are not suitable as they tend to be blown away. The protection can be removed when the old growth is cut back to soil level, as the new growth appears in the spring.

A final few words of warning: once established, hardies resent moving or having their roots disturbed, and as they are shallow rooters, any weeding should be done by hand, not hoe.

□ SPRING and FUCHSIA DORMANCY

One of the problems with the hardy fuchsia bed is the lack of interest during the period from late autumn to late spring. The interplanting of spring-flowering bulbs and wallflowers would need little labour and at the same time, afford some winter protection. Dwarf conifers would not crowd out the fuchsias, yet many require similar conditions. Other dwarf-growing evergreen shrubs together with hardy hebes could be considered.

□ COTTAGE GARDENS

Hardy fuchsias make a good display when associated with the old-fashioned cottage garden, the heyday of which coincided roughly with the Victorian era. Cottage-garden characteristics were colour and fragrance coupled with joyous abandon, suggesting nature running riot and the hardy fuchsia by the kitchen door fitted into this picture extemely well. One unusual fuchsia happened to have been found recently growing in a Devon cottage garden by a London busman on holiday. Enquiring after the name from the owners, the reply came that the name was not known but it had been growing in the garden for almost fifty years. Obtaining a plant, it was subsequently identified by a fuchsia expert as the long-lost 'Empress of Prussia'. One of our best hardies, it produces six and more flowers from the leaf axil.

In the cottage garden, pinks, wall-flowers, sweet williams, stocks, pot marigolds, love-in-a-mist are but a few possible companions, following on with the sweet clove-scented dianthus and clove carnations. Herbs provide material for sachets and pot-pourris; lavender springs immediately to mind, as do rosemary, mint, thyme and sage. Roses are a classic feature of the cottage garden while over the walls *Clematis montana rubens* with *Jasminum officinale* can play a prominent part.

□ FUCHSIAS AS HEDGES

It is doubtful whether the fuchsia as a hardy plant, especially grown as a hedge, has ever been utilized to its full potential. Provided they are not planted in a frost pocket, hardy fuchsias should survive almost everywhere; of course they grow most strongly in milder districts. Many fuchsia enthusiasts may have been influenced by witnessing the hedgerows of Devon and Cornwall, the west coast of Scotland, and in County Kerry on the west coast of Ireland, which include the species *F. magellanica* with its variants *alba (molinea), globosa, gracilis, riccartonii* and *thompsonii*, all of which have naturalized themselves in those parts of the world and flower from midsummer to early autumn.

The fuchsia can be used as a low hedge, for edging or dividing purposes and, if the suitable cultivars are selected, a sizeable screen or hedge can be grown.

Hardies for hedges will grow in most soils but good preparation of the site is necessary before actual planting. Fuchsias, although shallow rooters, need a deep, cool root run and preparation will mean deep digging to break up the subsoil. Should this subsoil be loose, the addition of material such as peat or humus of some description is necessary. If, on the other hand, the subsoil is clay or of a heavy nature, gravel or sand will be needed to prevent waterlogging. If farmyard manure is obtainable, this should be worked into the bottom spit. When returning the first spit, any moisture-retaining material such as peat, spent hops, humus or manure can be used to advantage.

Late autumn or early winter would be the ideal time to make this initial preparation, to allow the soil to weather before planting. The actual planting should take place as soon as the danger of frosts has disappeared – by late spring in mild areas, or early summer in colder regions. It would be advisable to order your plants from the nurseryman well in advance and to take delivery in pots no smaller than 9cm (3½in). Remember that nowadays we can obtain hardy plants in colours other than red and purple. Should you have the necessary facilities to grow the plants on to 11 or 12cm (4½ or 5in) pots then success will be greatly increased. But attention must be paid to ensure that whenever the plants are planted out, they have been successfully hardened off, otherwise the young plants' growth will be badly checked, the foliage turning bronzy and leaves falling off. Transfer the plants, in their pots, to a suitable garden frame, two or three weeks prior to planting. Gradually increase ventilation to a stage when the top light can be removed entirely, except for the nights when frosts can be expected.

Planting distances will vary according to the vigour of the cultivars, but generally 45cm (18in) is a good spacing distance. The depth of planting is important and plants should be set at least 5cm (2in) below the soil level to protect those vital roots from subsequent frost damage. Planting should be firm, with no air pockets – the heel of the boot trodden lightly around the plants is quite sufficient. No fertilizer or feeding is necessary at this time, although a little bonemeal dug in around the roots will be beneficial. Although fuchsias are gross feeders only moderate feeding should be carried out during the first summer, commencing with a weak feed with the concentration upon nitrogen, some three or four weeks after planting.

(Above) *A prolific-flowering standard of 'Phyllis' in a Chester garden, set off by large-flowered begonias.*

(Opposite) *The graceful long-tubed flowers of the old cultivar 'Mrs Rundle'.*

Fortnightly feeds in the same concentration can then be carried out during the growing season.

During the first winter it would be advantageous to cover the base of the plants with some protective material such as peat, sand, leaves or weathered ashes to protect the roots from any likely frosts and then remove it in the spring.

No pruning should be undertaken in the autumn or during the first winter, leaving all the growth made during the summer intact; this will give a certain amount of protection against any unkind weather. In any case most of the growth will be lost. Pruning should take place when the new growth appears at the base of the plants in the early or late spring. Either prune right down to ground level or to those shoots or eyes that appear a little way up the stems or laterals.

It will be in the second summer that the hedge will realize the growth and colour expected. Feeding can be stepped up considerably during this second year, first with the nitrogen feed and then switching over as buds and flowers appear to a feed with the emphasis on the potash content.

An incomplete list of cultivars suitable for growing as hedges include the following: 'Brilliant', 75 cm (2½ ft); 'Caledonia', 60 cm (2 ft); 'Chillerton Beauty', 60–90 cm (2–3 ft); 'Cliff's Hardy', 75 cm (2½ ft); 'Corallina', 90 cm (3 ft); 'Drame', 60 cm (2 ft); 'Dr Foster', 1 m (3½ ft); 'Enfant Prodigue', 90 cm (3 ft); 'Flash', 75 cm (2½ ft); 'Florence Turner', 90 cm (3 ft); 'Graf Witte', 90 cm (3 ft); 'Joan Cooper', 90 cm (3 ft); 'Madame Cornelissen', 90 cm (3 ft); *F. magellanica* var. *alba*, 1.8–3 m (6–10 ft); *F. m.* var. *gracilis*, 1.2–1.5 m (4–5 ft); *F. m.* var. *riccartonii*, 1.2–1.8 m (4–6 ft); *F. m.* var. *thompsonii*, 1.2–1.5 m (4–5 ft); 'Margaret', 90 cm–1.2 m (3–4 ft); 'Margaret Brown', 60–90 cm (2–3 ft); 'Mrs Popple', 60–90 cm (2–3 ft); 'Mrs W. P. Wood', 1.2–1.5 m (4–5 ft); 'Phyllis', 90 cm (3 ft); 'Pixie', 60–90 cm (2–3 ft); 'Prosperity', 90 cm (3 ft); 'Whiteknight's Blush', 90 cm (3 ft); 'Whiteknight's Pearl', 1.5 m (5 ft); 'White Pixie', 90 cm (3 ft). Should a box hedge or a very low hedge be required then both 'Lady Thumb' and 'Tom Thumb' at 30 cm (1 ft) could be considered.

DISPLAYS UNDER GLASS

Brilliant displays of colour can be obtained by growing fuchsias, associated with a wide range of other plants, under glass, whether in a cool greenhouse or a conservatory. This permits the enjoyment of plants throughout the year, but the question of how best to utilize your glasshouse depends on how the plants are mixed. One thing to bear in mind is not to grow too many plants and to select those plants which require more or less the same conditions. As fuchsias require a moist atmosphere, with plenty of shade and humidity, it would not be advisable to include, say cacti, carnations or orchids, which require different conditions. Temperatures should be a minimum of around 4–7°C (40–45°F), with an average, we could say, of 16°C (60°F), although most plants will suffer no great harm if the sun pushes the temperature up to 27°C (80°F). If the structure is both large enough and high enough, consider climbing plants, either grown in large pots or in the border. Climbers have the advantage of furnishing the upper part of the house and at the same time providing some shade in the summer when most needed. For a smallish house I would suggest fuchsia cultivars 'Muriel', 'Joan Smith' or 'Rose of Castile'; train up on one stem by pinching out all side shoots until the eaves are reached. Allow the plants to make natural growth in the summer and spur back to the main branches in winter. For other climbing shrubs I would suggest *Jasminum polyanthum* for the winter, *Passiflora caerulea* (passion flower) for the summer or *Solanum jasminoides* (Chilean potato flower) as a late-flowering species. A very short list of fuchsias best suited for greenhouse display could include the upright 'Annabel', 'Border Queen', 'Countess of Aberdeen', 'Estelle Marie', 'Heidi Ann', 'Joy Patmore', 'Lady Isobel Barnett', 'Royal Velvet' and 'Snowcap'. The *triphyllas* must include 'Thalia' and the new 'John Maynard Scales'. Should you want a species or two, then *F. fulgens* var. *rubra grandiflora* and *F. denticulata* will excel. The best of the trailing cultivars include 'Cascade', 'Marinka', 'Orange Drops', 'Pink Galore', 'Seventh Heaven' and 'Walsingham', whether in hanging pots or in baskets. On the solid staging benches, the tuberous begonias produce exotic blooms and together with gloxinias are among the most colourful flowers for summer and autumn; both these subjects love exactly the same conditions as fuchsias. *Begonia rex* is happier in fairly heavy shade and will do well under the staging. Impatiens and streptocarpus are both continuous summer-flowering subjects, and both extremely easy to cultivate. Coleus are popular subjects for their diversity of foliage colour and form; though named varieties are still perpetuated by cuttings, modern seed now produces a remarkable range of different colours. *Saintpaulia ionantha*, popularly known as African violets, do best in a warm greenhouse until reaching flowering size when they can be kept cooler. For the mixed house you cannot be without the adiantums, the maidenhair ferns, which are easily grown and add a foil to the potted fuchsias. I always include a few lilies in my fuchsia house, both for perfume and beauty, finding *Lilium auratum* and *L. speciosum* such excellent and easy subjects. Hydrangeas are first-class plants for the cool greenhouse, whilst camellias give me a wonderful display of colour in the early months of the year, particularly the hybrid variety 'Donation'. Although not mixing particularly well, pelargoniums, both the regal and the zonal varieties, flower extremely well. They do, however, prefer the atmosphere drier than fuchsias.

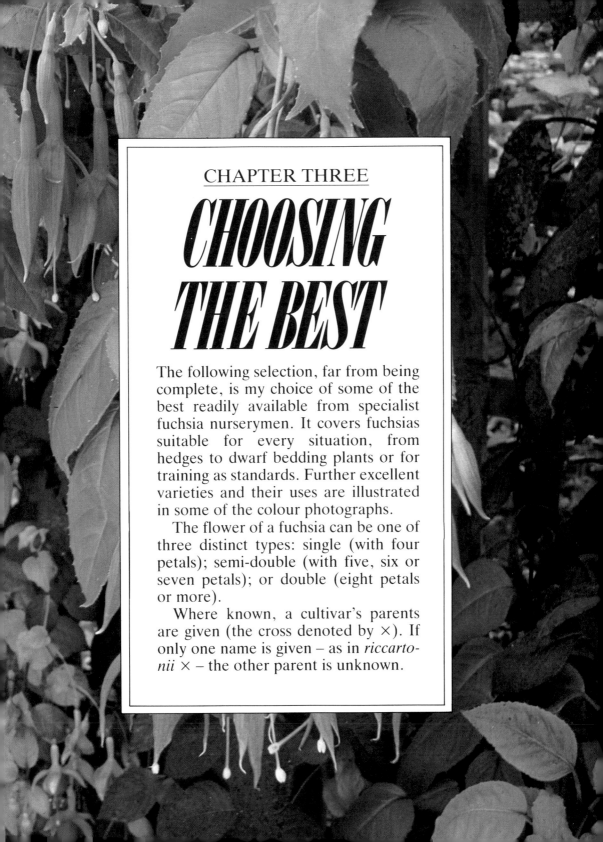

CHAPTER THREE

CHOOSING THE BEST

The following selection, far from being complete, is my choice of some of the best readily available from specialist fuchsia nurserymen. It covers fuchsias suitable for every situation, from hedges to dwarf bedding plants or for training as standards. Further excellent varieties and their uses are illustrated in some of the colour photographs.

The flower of a fuchsia can be one of three distinct types: single (with four petals); semi-double (with five, six or seven petals); or double (eight petals or more).

Where known, a cultivar's parents are given (the cross denoted by ×). If only one name is given – as in *riccartonii* × – the other parent is unknown.

DESCRIPTIVE LIST OF SELECTED SPECIES AND CULTIVARS

Readers are requested to note that at the end of each description the raiser's name has been quoted, together with nationality and date of introduction.

'ABBÉ FARGES'
Semi-double. Tube and reflexed sepals, light cerise; corolla rosy-lilac, flowers small but profuse. Small, medium green foliage, stems rather brittle and easily broken. Awarded HC by RHS in 1965 hardy trials. Growth upright, bushy and hardy.
Lemoine – French – 1901

'ACHIEVEMENT'
Single. Tube and recurved sepals, reddish cerise; corolla reddish purple, scarlet at base, bright and effective, beautiful shape. Flowers medium to large and very free. Foliage yellowish green, growth upright, bushy and self branching. Hardy and good for standard.
Melville – British – 1886

'ALICE HOFFMAN'
Semi-double. Tube and sepals rose; corolla white, veined rose. Flowers are small but very profuse, small foliage of bronzy green colour. Growth upright, compact and bushy, height 45–60 cm (1½–2 ft). Hardy.
Klese – German – 1911

F. alpestris
See *F. regia* var. *alpestris*.

'AMY LYE'
Single. Tube waxy cream, sepals white, tipped green; corolla coral orange, medium-sized blooms very free and early. Foliage dark green with crimson mid-rib. Growth very vigorous, best described as spreading, lax bush, needs early stopping. Good for standard and all tall training, also as half-hardy bedder.
Lye – British – 1885

'ANNABEL'
Double. The white tube is rather long and striped pink, long broadish sepals are white slightly flushed pink, which curl at the tips and are recurved, held well out from the tube, pink at base. The white double corolla is veined pink, long and very full, very free flowering for a double cultivar, lightish green foliage. The growth is upright but although inclined to be lax is strong enough to carry the heavy blooms which hang in clusters. Good as half-hardy bedder.
Ryle – British – 1977

'ANN HOWARD TRIPP'
Single to semi-double. Short thick white tube with faint stripe, white sepals held at the horizontal, edged and tinged with palest pink, tipped green. Corolla white, very lightly veined pink held well clear of foliage. Produces two flowers in each leaf axil, exceptionally free-flowering. Pale green foliage, leaves of new growth yellow, changing with maturity. Growth upright, very vigorous and self-branching. Half-hardy bedder.
'Lady Isobel Barnett' × 'Joy Patmore'.
Clark (Merseyside) – British – 1982

'BASHFUL'

Double. Tube and sepals deep pink; corolla white, veined red. Small blooms, very free, deep green foliage. Growth upright and bushy, strong and stiff. Dwarf, only 23–37 cm (9–15 in) high, hardy. Good for the rockery or edging. Tabraham – British – 1974

'BEACON'

Single. Tube and sepals, deep pink; corolla bright mauvish pink. Medium-sized flowers, very free. Darkish green foliage with waved edges. Growth upright, bushy and compact. Good as half-hardy bedder.
Bull – British – 1871

'BLANCHE REGINA'

Double. Tube and sepals white, sepals are reflexed, crepe on inside. Corolla amethyst-violet, changing to rhodamine-purple with age. Medium-sized blooms, very free and continuous. Good for baskets. Growth self-branching, natural trailer. 'La Campanella' × 'Flirtation Waltz'.
Clyne – British – 1974

'BON ACCORDE'

Single. One of the most unusual cultivars as its delicate blooms stand out erect. This charming cultivar was raised by the Frenchman Crousse in 1861. Tube and sepals are waxy, ivory white and the corolla of a delicate pale purple, suffused white, exceptionally free-flowering and small in size. Growth is bushy and very upright. Will make a delightful quarter- or half-standard, especially when used as an outside bedder as a 'dot' plant. One of the finest beds of half-standards of 'Bon Accorde' is to be seen at Chester Zoo.
Crousse – French – 1861

'BORDER QUEEN'

Single. Short thin tube, sepals rhodamine-pink tipped pea green, underside neyron-rose, veins darker rose, flare out with tips turned up. Corolla amethyst-violet, flushed pale pink with dark pink veins, fading to white at base, bell shaped. Foliage medium green, stems reddish, leaves smooth. Growth upright and self branching, good as half-hardy bedder. 'Leonora' × 'Lena Dalton'.
Ryle – British – 1974

'BRUTUS'

Single. Short tube and recurving sepals, rich cerise; corolla rich dark purple, ageing to reddish purple. Medium-sized flowers, very profuse and early bloomer. Growth upright, vigorous and bushy. Versatile for all types of training. One of the very good old cultivars, hardy in most parts.
Lemoine – French – 1897

'CARDINAL FARGES'

Semi-double. Tube and reflexed sepals, pale cerise; corolla white, lightly veined cerise. Flowers are quite small but profuse. Growth upright, bushy and vigorous, similar to and a sport of 'Abbé Farges', has the same small fault – rather brittle growth. Hardy.
Rawlins – British – 1958

'CELIA SMEDLEY'

Single. Neyron-rose tube and sepals, whilst the corolla is a vivid currant red, flowers larger than average, but freely

(Opposite) *'Amy Marie' is the classic red and white fuchsia, as near perfect as you could expect. A natural trailer that makes a striking basket.*

(Above) *Semi-double 'Ann H. Tripp' is one of our best whites, always in bloom. Can be late into flower.*

(Left) *The superb white and dark rose cultivar 'Arabella' was introduced in 1866, yet is still grown.*

produced, largish leaves of medium green. Growth is extremely vigorous and produces an excellent bush or bedder. Makes a magnificent tub speciment for the patio, a third-year plant with good cultivation can obtain a width and height of over 1.2 m (4 ft). 'Joy Patmore' × 'Glitters'.
Bellamy raised, introduced by Roe – British – 1970

'CHANG'
Single. Tube orange-red, sepals orange-red, tipped green, paler underneath; corolla brilliant orange. Flowers are small but profuse. Growth upright bush and vigorous, must be stopped frequently in early stages. Good for standard or bedder. Flowers better out of doors. *F. cordifolia* hybrid.
Hazard and Hazard – American – 1946

'CHARMING'
Single. Tube carmine, sepals reddish cerise, well reflexed, corolla rosy-purple, cerise at base. Foliage slightly yellowish, very light at tips of leaf. Medium-sized flowers, very free. Growth upright bushy and hardy. 'Arabella Improved' × 'James Lye'.
Lye – British – 1895

'CHECKERBOARD'
Single. Long tube red, sepals slightly recurved, start red and change abruptly to white. Corolla red but deeper than tube, white at base. Flowers are long and of medium size, blooms drop very quickly but hardly noticed with the great profusion; flowers very early and always in bloom. Growth upright and vigorous. Will produce good standard or bedder.
Walker and Jones – American – 1948

'CHILLERTON BEAUTY'
Single. Tube and sepals, pale rose pink, tipped green; corolla mauvish violet slightly veined pink. Small flowers but very free, growth upright and bushy. Suitable cultivar for a medium-sized hedge with a height of about 1 m (3 ft). Named after Chillerton, Isle of Wight.
Bass – British – 1847

'CLOVERDALE JEWEL'
Semi-double. Tube and sepals held well back to tube, neyron-rose. Corolla wisteria blue with rose veining, passing to violet-blue. Medium-sized blooms, very floriferous, early flowerer. Good for standard work especially the miniature. Growth upright and bushy. 'Cloverdale' × 'Lady Isobel Barnett'.
Gadsby – British – 1974

'CLOVERDALE PEARL'
Single. White tube, sepals rhodamine-pink, shading to white, tipped green, curving back towards tube. Corolla white of medium size and well formed, free bloomer. Self-branching bush. Good for all types of standards and as bedder. Unnamed seedling × 'Grace Darling'.
Gadsby – British – 1974

'COACHMAN'
Single. Tube and sepals, pale salmon; corolla rich orange-vermilion. Beautiful clear colouring. Medium-sized blooms, very free and early, blooms in flushes. Vigorous, lax growth, excels as a half-basket.
Bright – British – 1910

'CONSTANCE'
Double. Tube and sepals, soft pink; corolla bluish mauve, tinted pink. Medium-sized blooms, very free, very similar to 'Pink Pearl' from which it is a seedling, except the corolla is of different colouring. Growth upright and bushy, very easy; better as second-year plant. Hardy.
Berkeley Hort. Nursery – America – 1935

'COUNTESS OF ABERDEEN'

Single. Tube and sepals, very pale pink; corolla creamy white flushed pale pink, very pale pink in shade almost white, but rich pink in full sun. Small blooms but very profuse. Growth upright and bushy but rather stiff. Half-hardy bedder and also good for small standards. Capable of magnificent specimens.
Dobbie Forbes – British – 1888

'DISPLAY'

Single. Almost a self pink, tube and sepals are rose pink whilst the corolla is of a deeper pink. One of the best all-round fuchsias in cultivation, capable of being trained to any shape, except a basket; excels as a bush plant, but makes an excellent standard. One of the few that can be grown in the house, provided it receives full light and atmosphere not too dry. One of the first to flower and continues to bloom, without flushes, throughout the entire season. With its vigorous root system is one of the best types for bedding out and, although not classified as a hardy, will stand all but the worst of winters.
Smith – British – 1881

'DOLLAR PRINCESS'

Double. Tube and sepals cerise; corolla rich purple. Flowers rather small for a double, but very profuse and of perfect shape, very early bloomer. Growth upright and vigorous, excels as bush plant but can be trained to almost all shapes, particularly good for standards and bedder. One of the real old cultivars which any grower can cultivate with ease. Very often named backwards as 'Princess Dollar'.
Lemoine – French – 1912

'DRAME'

Semi-double. Tube and sepals scarlet; corolla violet-purple. Medium-sized blooms and very free, with yellowish green foliage. Growth upright bushy and spreading. Hardy, suitable for low hedge up to 60 cm (2 ft). _riccartonii_ ×.
Lemoine – French – 1880

'DR FOSTER'

Single. Tube and sepals scarlet; corolla violet. Large flowers and free. Growth upright and bushy, hardy. The outstanding feature of this cultivar is that it is probably the largest flower for a hardy, suitable for a low hedge of up to 90 cm (3 ft).
Lemoine – French – 1899

'DUSKY BEAUTY'

Single. Tube and horizontally held sepals neyron-rose. Corolla pale purple with pink cast and deeper pink edges. Small flowers very prolific, best colour in shade. Medium to dark green foliage, ovate with obtuse leaf tip. Grows as small upright but will also make a good bush.
Ryle – British – 1981

'ELIZABETH'

Single. Very long tube, rose-opal, sepals rose-opal, tipped green; corolla deep rich rose with salmon-pink shading. Long slender flowers and free, very similar to 'Mrs W. Rundle', but 'Elizabeth' growth is more vigorous. Growth upright, will make a greenhouse climber.
Whiteman – British – 1941

(Above) *'Celia Smedley' is a vigorous cultivar with distinct currant-red blooms.*

(Opposite) *'Countess of Aberdeen' is unmatched for beauty.*

'EMPRESS OF PRUSSIA'
Single. Tube and sepals glowing scarlet; corolla reddish magenta, paler at base. Largish flowers for a hardy, and very free; outstanding feature is that every joint carries six to eight blooms instead of the customary two. Growth upright and bushy up to 90 cm (3 ft), one of the outstanding hardy cultivars. Found in 1958 growing in a garden where it had been for over fifty years. Raiser's name thought to be lost in the realms of antiquity at the time Bernard Rawlins reintroduced.
Hoppe – British – 1868

'ESTELLE MARIE'
Single. Tube greenish white, short and thick. Sepals white with very prominent green tips, standing straight up. Corolla opens blue-violet, matures to violet with white at base of petals. Four petals form a cup with overlap. Foliage dark green leaves oval and of good substance. Growth upright and sturdy, self-branching with typical 'Bon Accorde' habit of carrying flowers erect. Makes exceptionally good half-hardy bedder. Considered to be of 'Bon Accorde' descendancy.
Newton – American – 1973

'FALLING STARS'
Single. Tube and pleated sepals pale
scarlet; corolla turkey-red with slight
orange tint. Perfectly shaped flowers,
very clean appearance, very free.
Growth lax upright, needs a lot of early
pinching, excels as a half-basket, will
produce a good standard. 'Morning
Mist' × 'Cascade'.
Reiter – American – 1941

'FLASH'
Single. Tube and sepals light magenta-
red, almost a self. Flowers are small.
Growth upright and bushy up to 75 cm
(2½ft), very vigorous, can be grown to
very large specimen plants. Suitable as a
low hedge, hardy in most districts.
Hazard and Hazard – American – 1930?

F. fulgens
Long tube. Light vermilion-red, sepals
yellowish to greenish with red base;
corolla bright vermilion. Extremely
attractive flowers, very long, pendulous
and borne at the extreme ends of the
branches in long and lasting clusters.
Foliage is light sage green, darker on
upper sides, large with hairy leaves; the
largest of any known fuchsia, measuring
some 23 cm (9 in). One of the species
with thickened tuberous roots. Upright
shrub up to 1.2 m (4ft). Described as the
aristocrat of the genus.
De Candolle – Mexico – 1828
Both the variants below are excellent as
half-hardy bedders, but they are very
frost-shy.
var. *gesneriana*
Similar flowers but habit of growth is
rather lax with shorter flower tube.
Native to Guatemala.

var. *rubra grandiflora*
Very long-tubed flowers with similar
habit of growth, but the most beautiful.
Native to Guatemala and Salvador.

'GARDEN NEWS'
Double. Short thick, pink tube, sepals
pink on outside and frosty rose pink.
Broad, short and of good substance,
well arched from base of corolla.
Corolla is shades of magenta-rose, base
of petals rose pink. Large blooms of
attractive shape, mainly in fours at each
pair of leaf axils. Continuous flowering.
Mid-green foliage, lightly serrated.
Grows to a tall, upright bush with large
proportion of three-leaved stems, self
branching. Will make good bush or
decorative, will take full sun where
colour best develops. Hardy.
Handley – British – 1978

'GARTENMEISTER BONSTEDT'
Triphylla single. Long tube, orange
brick-red self, very free. Flowers are
almost identical to 'Thalia', the
distinguishing feature separating the
two is the pronounced bulge in the tube
of 'Gartenmeister'. Foliage dark bronzy
red. Growth upright and very vigorous,
will stand sun and heat and makes
wonderful half-hardy bedder but very
frost-shy. *F. triphylla* ×.
Bonstedt – German – 1905

'GENII'
Single. Tube and sepals cerise; corolla
rich violet, ageing to dark rose. Small
flowers, very free, small foliage light
yellowish green with red stems. Growth
upright and bushy, grows better outside,
under glass difficult to control and may

drop buds and flowers. When first introduced was known as 'Jeane'. One of the few ornamental hardies.
Reiter – American – 1951

'GRAF WITTE'
Single. Tube and sepals carmine; corolla purple shaded rosy mauve. Very small flowers, but profuse. Yellowish green foliage with crimson mid-rib and veins. Grows to a medium bush to 90 cm (3 ft), ideal as a permanent bedder. Hardy.
Lemoine – French – 1899

'HARRY GRAY'
Double. Rose pink streaked tube fairly short, slightly recurved sepals white, shading to rose pink at the base, tipped green. Corolla white shading to rose pink at base changing to very pale pink with maturity. Small to medium-sized blooms, very full but compact like a small powder puff, very prolific for a double. Dark green foliage small and short-jointed, ovate with red stems. Growth self-branching trailer or lax upright, makes a wonderful dense basket, best colour in filtered shade. 'La Campanella' × 'Powder Puff'.
Dunnett – British – 1981

'HEIDI ANN'
Double. Tube and sepals, crimson-cerise; corolla bright lilac, paler at base, veined cerise. Flowers medium-sized, very free and of perfect shape, similar to 'Mauve Beauty'. Dark green foliage with crimson mid-rib. Growth upright and bushy, needs and responds to early pinching. Good as half-hardy bedder. 'Tennessee Waltz' × 'General Monk'.
Smith (Mrs) – British – 1969

'HIDCOTE BEAUTY'
Single. Tube and sepals waxy cream, tipped green; corolla pale salmon pink, shaded light rose. Flowers medium-sized and free, of clean bright appearance. Light green foliage. Growth upright and bushy, versatile in training, makes stately standard and with careful cultivation a good basket subject. Good as half-hardy bedder.
Webb – British – 1949

'JACK ACLAND'
Single. Tube and sepals, bright pink; corolla deep rose, ageing to almost same colour as sepals. Large flowers, very free bloomer and fat buds. Growth fairly upright and bushy, with careful training can produce good standard. Although rather stiff will produce magnificent basket 1.2-1.5 m (4–5 ft) across by midsummer.
Haag and Son – American – 1952

'JACK SHAHAN'
Single. Tube and sepals, pale rose-bengal, corolla rose-bengal. Large flowers and very free, growth inclined to be lax but makes a fine bush plant. With care can be trained as a good weeping standard. Also makes a good basket.
Tiret – American – 1948

'JAMES LYE'
Double. Tube and sepals cerise; corolla bluish mauve, flushed pale mauve at base. Medium-sized flowers, very free, perfect shaped bloom, similar to 'Constance' but darker. Growth upright and bushy, ideal cultivar for tall training and a good half-hardy bedder.
Lye – British – 1883

'JEANE'
See Genii.

'JOAN SMITH'
Single. Tube and reflexing sepals, flesh pink; corolla soft pink with a touch of cerise. Medium-sized flowers, very early and free but colouring can be very disappointing, very pale. The outstanding feature of this cultivar is the growth, probably the fastest to date – strong upright, vigorous, will reach several feet on current growth, difficult to control. Ideal growth for a climber.
Thorne – British – 1958

'JOY PATMORE'
Single. Short white tube, pure waxy white sepals, spreading and upturned, reverse side white with a faint pink reflection from the corolla. Corolla, startling shade of rich carmine difficult to describe. Medium-sized flowers, very free, when flower is fully open the white centre is most attractive. Growth upright and bushy. Will produce good standard or bedder.
Turner – British – 1961

'LA CAMPANELLA'
Semi-double. This cultivar was a chance seedling rather than a deliberate cross. The sepals are white, slightly flushed pink, while the corolla is a beautiful shade of imperial purple and has a delightful colour change to lavender as the blooms age. This is a very floriferous cultivar, flowers are small, but exceptionally profuse. When fully established in a large basket, you can lose twenty odd blooms a day and not notice. The easiest of cultivars to

propagate, will make good quarter- or half-standard and worth considering as an espalier.
Blackwell – British – 1968

'LADY ISOBEL BARNETT'
Single. Sepals and tube are rosy red, whilst the open-type corolla, where the blood of 'Caroline' is detected, is rose-purple with edges of flushed imperial purple. Blooms are of smallish to medium size. Makes a medium-sized bush and upright, which carries its flowers semi-erect with eight or more blooms from the leaf axils. 'Lady Isobel Barnett' is one of the most prolific bloomers to date, will stand moderate sun. Will produce a fine standard and a good half-hardy bedder. Excels as a bush plant, magnificent trained as a conical and good specimens can be breathtaking. 'Caroline' × 'Derby Belle'.
Gadsby – British – 1968

'LADY THUMB'
Semi-double. Tube and sepals reddish-light carmine; corolla white, slightly veined carmine. Very small flowers, extremely free which tend to drop rather quickly like its parent, 'Tom Thumb'. Very small foliage; growth dwarf, upright and hardy. Ultimate height is only 30 cm (12 in); good for front row or edging.
Roe – British – 1966

'LAKESIDE'
Single. The tube and sepals are reddish

(Opposite) 'Dancing Flame' from California makes a superb basket display.

pink with green tips, whilst the corolla is bluish violet, veined bright pink and as the blooms mature, fades to lilac. Filament and style are pink; plant has attractive foliage of medium green with small leaves. Growth is definitely of cascade habit. 'Lakeside' is extremely vigorous and self-branching and would make a fine quarter- or half-standard, but excels when grown as a full basket.
Thornley – British – 1967

'LENA'
Semi-double. Tube and half-reflexed sepals, pale flesh pink, slightly deeper underneath; corolla rosy magenta, flushed pink, paling at base. Medium-sized flowers, very free, blooms in flushes. One of the most versatile of cultivars, can be trained to almost any shape. Lena is hardy and will make a good basket.
Bunney – British – 1862

'LEONORA'
Single. Very soft pink self, flowers of medium size, extremely floriferous, bell-shaped, probably the best self pink to date. Growth upright, vigorous and bushy, will produce half-hardy bedder.
Tiret – American – 1960

'LINDISFARNE'
Semi-double. The short, thick tube is the palest of pinks, sepals held horizontally are also pale pink, flushed darker pink at the edges and tip. Corolla a rich dark violet, deeper at the edges, flushed palish pink at the base. Flowers are rather small but prolific and a blue which seems to hold its colour without fading. Can best be described as an

upright 'La Campanella', a strong grower with self-branching habit. Will make a fine standard and a useful half-hardy bedder.
Ryle – British – 1974

'LYE'S UNIQUE'
Single. Tube and sepals waxy white; corolla delightful shade of salmon orange. Medium-sized blooms very free. Growth upright, very strong. One of Lye's best. Bedder or standard.
Lye – British – 1886

'MADAME CORNELISSEN'
Semi-double. Tube and sepals rich scarlet; corolla white, veined cerise. Smallish flowers but extremely free, dark green foliage. Growth, strong, upright and bushy, hardy and suitable for hedges, height 90 cm (3 ft).
Cornelissen – Belgian – 1860

F. magellanica
Red tube, deep red sepals, purple corolla. Small flowers, very free, the hardiest of all fuchsias and has played an important role in the evolution of the present fuchsia, being extensively used by the early hybridists. There are numerous forms and natural variants which are themselves amongst the hardiest of fuchsias.
Lamark – Chile and Argentina – 1768
var. *alba*
Synonymous with *molinae*, below.
var. *molinae*
Probably the best known and widely grown as *F.m.* var. *alba*. Small flowers with white tube and very pale lilac sepals and corolla. Very hardy, will produce a hedge 1.8–3 m (6–10 ft) high.

var. *gracilis*

Flowers are slightly longer with deep purple corolla, habit of more slender growth but rampant and arching. Extremely hardy, producing a hedge up to 1.5 m (5 ft).

var. *gracilis variegata*

Identical to *F.m.* var. *gracilis* but with silvery variegated foliage. One of the few hardy ornamentals, capable of hedge up to 1.5 m (5 ft).

var. *riccartonii*

Probably the best known of hardy fuchsias. The name may sound of Spanish origin but originated from a garden at Riccarton, near Edinburgh. The flowers are single, tube and sepals scarlet, with dark purple corolla, very long narrow sepals recurved and held well below the horizontal; prolific with bloom, long for size with bronze to reddish cast on the foliage. In spring, fresh young shoots appear from the base. These grow 1.2–1.5 m (4–5 ft) tall and bear the familiar drooping turkey-red and purple blooms, so aptly named lady's eardrops. Extremely hardy, will produce hedge up to 1.8 m (6 ft).

var. *thompsonii*

With very bright coloured flowers, tube and sepals scarlet, corolla palish purple. Hardy in all districts. Will make hedge up to 1.5 m (5 ft).

var. *tricolor*

Single. Tube and sepals crimson; corolla purple, cerise at base. Small flowers, very free. Variegated foliage of cream and green with pink flush. Growth upright, bushy and hardy, suitable as hedge with height up to 90 cm (3 ft). Lower growing than *F.m.* var. *gracilis* *variegata* and flowers later. *F. magellanica* var. *gracilis variegata* ×. Potney – British – Date unknown

'MARGARET'

Semi-double. Tube and sepals carmine-scarlet, corolla violet, veined cerise. Medium-sized flowers, large for hardy, very free when established. Growth upright, bushy and vigorous, suitable for hedge, height up to 1.2 m (4 ft), very hardy. *F. magellanica* var. *alba* × 'Heritage'.
Wood – British – 1937 or 1943

'MARGARET ROE'

Single. Tube and sepals rosy red; corolla pale violet-purple. medium-sized blooms, very free, held upright. Growth upright bushy, hardy, makes excellent bedder. 'Caroline' × 'Derby Belle'.
Gadsby – British – 1968

'MARIN GLOW'

Single. The tube and sepals are pure waxy white, whilst the corolla is rich imperial purple, ageing slowly to magenta and while in its prime, seems to be almost phosphorescent. The blooms are of medium size and extremely profuse, of a classic fuchsia shape. Medium green foliage is clean. The growth is strong and upright, develops into a shapely bush without much attention. It is vigorous and self-branching. Although mainly grown as a bush plant, will develop into an excellent half- or full-standard. Will develop into an excellent half-hardy bedder for the summer.
Reedstrom – American – 1954

(Opposite) *'Flirtation Waltz' is beautiful and easy to grow but it bruises easily.*
(Above) *'Grüss aus dem Bodethal' has an intense dark colouring.*

'MARINKA'

Single. Tube and sepals rich red; corolla slightly darker red, almost a self. Medium-sized flowers, extremely profuse, has the appearance of a semi-double, beautifully shaped. Growth a vigorous cascade, versatile for all types of training except bush. Has become the standard upon which all baskets are judged.
Rozain-Boucharlat – French – 1902

'MEPHISTO'

Single. Tube and sepals scarlet; corolla deep crimson, almost a crimson self. Smallish flowers but extremely floriferous, borne in clusters, early. Growth is terrific, vigorous and rampant, no use under glass except as climber, makes a good bedder and hardy. *F. lycioides* × 'Mrs W. Rundle'. Reiter – American – 1941

'MICKY GOULT'

Single. Short white tube, short broad sepals, white on top, very pale pink underneath toning down to deeper pink, held at the horizontal and slightly tipped green. Short corolla, mallow purple with slight veining and lighter colour at edges. Small flowers, true single held semi-erect and do not fade even with maturity. Very early flowering, very

free and held in clusters. Light green foliage with ovate-cordate leaves. Growth very upright and bushy, neat and compact if frequently pinched. Will show up to advantage as a half-hardy bedder. 'Bobby Shaftoe' × 'Santa Barbara' (syn. 'Lustre').
Roe – British – 1981

'MIEKE MEURSING'
Single to semi-double. Was a chance seedling found growing on the staging under a plant of 'R.A.F.' by F. G. Hopwood at Hurstbourne Park, Hampshire in 1968. The sepals are red, whilst the corolla is pale pink with deeper veining and long stamens, extremely free flowering, but colouring can be dull and insipid. Its growth is exceptional, extremely vigorous and bushy, with a mass of growth from the base of the plant. Will make a fine standard and good bedder in the border.

'MR A. HUGGETT'
Single. Short tube is scarlet-cerise, sepals of the same colour are recurved and stand out horizontally while the nicely formed corolla is of mauvish pink with petals edged purple and pink at the base. The small foliage is in keeping with the strong, upright and bushy growth. An early flowerer, it continues to flower throughout the whole summer and one of the last to rest in the autumn. Very good as a bedder.
Raiser unknown – British – Date unknown

'MRS LOVELL SWISHER'
Single. Long tube flesh pink, sepals pinkish white, tipped green, deeper

pink underneath. Corolla deep old rose. Small flowers very profuse, similar to 'Checkerboard' but smaller, very early bloomer. Growth upright, very vigorous. Good in the border as a bedder in the border.
Jones – British – *circa.* 1862

'MRS MARSHALL'
Single. Tube and sepals waxy creamy white; corolla rosy cerise. Medium-sized flowers, very free, fairly early. Growth upright and bushy, very versatile for all shapes, will be seen to advantage as a bedder in the border.
Jones – British – 1862?

'MRS POPPLE'
Single. Tube and sepals scarlet; corolla purple-violet, cerise at centre, veined cerise. Medium-sized flowers, free, large for hardy cultivar. Growth upright, bushy and vigorous, very hardy. Makes a good hedge up to 90 cm (3 ft).
Elliott – British – 1899

'MRS W. P. WOOD'
Single. Tube and sepals pale pink; corolla pure white. Flowers very small but very profuse, small lightish green foliage. Growth upright and bushy, hardy. Selfed seedling from 'Margaret', and a hybrid from *F. magellanica* var. *alba*. Much too vigorous for cultivation under glass. Will produce hedge up to 1.5 m (5 ft).
Wood – British – 1949

'MRS (W.) RUNDLE'
Single. Very long tube and reflexed sepals flesh pink; corolla rich orange-vermilion. Flowers largish and long,

very free, features are the very long tube referred to as 'the epitome of grace and beauty'. Foliage lightish green. Grows to a lax bush, produces a magnificent weeping standard, or even a hanging basket. 'Earl of Beaconsfield' × 'Lady Heytesbury'.
Rundle – British – 1883

'MURIEL'
Semi-double. Long tube and sepals scarlet; corolla light purple veined cerise. Largish flowers, very free, not the brightest of colouring. Growth lax and cascading, extremely vigorous and very fast, suitable for greenhouse climber or weeping standard.
Raiser unknown – British – Date unknown

'NANCY LOU'
Double. Pale pink tube, sepals deep clear pink, turned right back. Corolla brilliant white. Large blooms of perfect shape, free for size. Growth upright.
Stubbs – American – 1971

'NORTHWAY'
Single. Short, thick tube light pink, short reflexed sepals, light pink. Corolla cherry red, nice break from the red and purple. Small flowers similar in shape to 'Lustre', very profuse. Small light green foliage. Growth rather lax but will produce bush or shrub without the need of supports. Suitable as miniature standard or as bedder. 'La Campanella' × 'Howlett's Hardy'.
Golics – British – 1976

'OTHER FELLOW'
Single. Tube and sepals waxy white, tipped green; corolla coral pink, white at base. Small flowers with profusion of bloom, very dainty. Growth upright and bushy. Exceptionally good cultivar. Good as standard.
Hazard and Hazard – American – 1946

'PACQUESA'
Single. Short deep red tube, reflexing sepals, deep red with crepe reverse; corolla pure white with faint trace of deep red veining. Largish flowers and extremely free, petals are of classic shape, very similar in shape to 'Ballet Girl'. Foliage parsley green with almond-shaped leaves, growth upright and bushy, self-branching, strong short-jointed habit. This is not just another red and white cultivar, but an improvement. Good as half-hardy bedder. 'Pacific Queen' × 'Sheryl Ann'.
Clyne – British – 1974

'PAPOOSE'
Semi-double. Tube and sepals bright red; corolla very dark purple. Small flowers, prolific, more flowers than foliage. Low bush, versatile for any type of training, delightful as half standard, will produce a fine basket. Hardy.
Reedstrom – American – 1960

'PHYLLIS'
Semi-double. Tube and sepals waxy rose flushed cerise; corolla rosy cerise. Produces sepals other than the normal four. Smallish flowers, very free and early. Growth an upright bush, extremely vigorous, no use for greenhouse, but ideal for large standards or pyramids. Very stiff growth, hardy, suitable for hedges up to 1–1.2 m (3–4 ft).
Brown – British – 1938

'PINK DARLING'
Single. Tube dark pink, sepals pale pink, deeper underneath; corolla soft lilac pink. Small flowers in great profusion, held semi-erect. Growth upright and bushy, will respond to the needed frequent pinching. Excellent cultivar in every way. Standard or bedder. .
Machado – American – 1961

'PINK GALORE'
Double. Cultivar most aptly named. The long tube and upturned sepals are slightly deeper pink than the corolla; the corolla itself is long, of a beautiful soft rose or candy pink, double, of long-lasting qualities, ideal for the planting of baskets. Foliage is excellent and unusual – dark glossy leaves; the young laterals are easily distinguished, having reddish stems. Makes a nice weeping standard, looks charming and delicate as a table or quarter-standard. Can be used as outside bedder. Delightful, elegant beauty and probably the best of the pinks.
Fuchsia-La – American – 1958

'PINK MARSHMALLOW'
Double. Tube and sepals pale pink, tipped green, blush pink underneath. Corolla white, blushed and veined pink, almost a self. Large blooms, free for size, sepals turn back and centre of corolla elongates to create double skirted effect, beautiful pastel shaded. Largish, light green foliage. Growth trailing, produces huge basket, whether half- or full.
Stubbs – American – 1971

(Opposite) *'Ian Leedham', a large semi-double*

'PINK PEARL'
Semi-double. Tube and incurved sepals pale pink; corolla deeper shade of pink slightly flushed rose. Medium-sized flowers, free, can come fully double. Growth upright. Very easy to grow and especially suitable for the training of standards and any tall type of training.
Bright – British – 1919

'PIXIE'
Single. Tube and sepals pale cerise; corolla rosy mauve, paler at base, veined carmine. Medium-sized flowers, very heavy bloomer. Foliage yellowish green with crimson veins. Growth upright, bushy and hardy. Vigorous, almost too vigorous for greenhouse, will produce a low hedge, height up to 90 cm (3 ft). Sport of 'Graf Witte'.
Russell – British – 1960

'PRESIDENT'
Single. Tube and sepals, bright red; corolla rosy magenta, scarlet at base. Medium-sized flowers, very free, dark green foliage with distinct red tint. Grows to an upright bush, very vigorous and hardy. One of the earliest of cultivars and still holds its own with modern cutivars. 'Formosa Elegans' × *F. corymbiflora*.
Standish – British – 1841

'PRESIDENT LEO BOULLEMIER'
Single. Short fluted tube streaked magenta; white flared sepals fairly long and pointed. Bell-shaped corolla magenta-blue maturing to blush pink. Medium-sized flowers of perfect shape and unusual colouring. Dark green foliage, pointed and with prominent

serrated edge. Growth upright and bushy, short-jointed especially when grown cool. Hardy in most districts, good as bedder. 'Joy Patmore' × 'Cloverdale Pearl'.
Burns – British – 1983

'PRESIDENT STANLEY WILSON'
Single. Tube colouring is carmine, sepals are carmine turning to pale pink and tipped green, while the corolla is rose carmine. Extremely free-flowering, has a long continuous production of buds, and is always in bloom, even in the late autumn. Foliage is medium green colour, fairly pest-free. Growth can be described as vigorous and strong with a natural trailing habit, will produce a magnificent basket. Will also produce a fine espalier in fan form and a good weeping standard. 'Brentwood' × 'Orange Drops'.
Thorne – British – 1968

'PRIDE OF THE WEST'
Single. Long tube and sepals palish red, sepals are narrow, upswept and slightly twisted. Corolla plum-red, flowers largish, free and long. Colour combination disappointing. Growth extremely vigorous, suitable as greenhouse climber, no use for pot work, almost as fast as 'Joan Smith'. Unusual cultivar for James Lye.
Lye – British – 1871

'PRINCESS DOLLAR'
See 'Dollar Princess'.

'PRINCESSITA'
Single. Tube and sepals white, gracefully curved; corolla deep rose. Medium-sized flowers and free. Growth

trailing. Will produce a fine basket. 'Fandango' × 'Mrs W. Rundle'.
Niederholzer – American – 1940

F. procumbens
This trailing species first discovered in 1834 in the North Island of New Zealand, growing in the sand along the shoreline. Prostrate in growth, the slender, trailing stems often attain several feet in length. Greenish yellow tube, red at base; sepals green, tipped purple; no corolla but the stamens bear bright blue pollen. The distinguishing characteristics are the erect flowers, only about 5 mm (¼ in) high, and the stigma which may appear above or below the level of the stamens. Seed pods, which are green turning to plum purple with maturity, are quite large and attractive. Flowers are very free, very small, point upwards, very unfuchsia-like. The foliage also cannot be recognized as a fuchsia's, very small leaves. This species is extremely hardy, can be used to effect on the larger rockeries or even very suitable for furnishing a hanging basket.
Cunningham – New Zealand – 1834

'PROSPERITY'
Double. Thick tube crimson, sepals crimson, waxy and firm; corolla pale neyron-rose, flushed and veined rose red. Medium-sized blooms, extremely free, fully double of good shape. Dark glossy green foliage, large leaves produced in threes at most joints. Growth upright, bushy and hardy, excels as outside bedder. 'Bishop's Bells' × 'Strawberry Delight'.
Gadsby – British – 1970

F. regia
Tube and sepals red; corolla darker red. Very small flowers, rampant climber attaining a height of 6 m (20 ft) in its natural habitat, with long and slender branches.
Gardner – Brazil – 1842

var. *alpestris*
Native of Organ Mountains in Brazil at elevation of 1500 m (5000 ft), flowers similar in colour and formation to the *magellanica* types, usually listed in nurserymen's catalogues as *F. alpestris*. Very suitable as a greenhouse climber.

'ROSE OF CASTILE'
Single. Tube and sepals waxy white, tipped green, bulging tube, sepals very faintly flushed pale pink. Corolla purple, faintly flushed rose, whitish at base. Smallish to medium flowers, free, beautiful colouring. Growth upright and bushy, hardy. Produces fine standard.
Banks – British – 1855

'ROSE OF CASTILE IMPROVED'
Single. Tube and sepals flesh pink; corolla violet-purple. Medium-sized flowers and free, blooms in flushes. Lightish green foliage, growth upright, bushy, hardy and vigorous. Very distinct from 'Rose of Castile' but no improvement, except that flowers are larger and growth more vigorous.
Banks – British – 1869

'RUFUS'
Single. Bright turkey-red self. Medium-sized flowers, extremely free, always in bloom. Growth upright and bushy, strong grower, excellent bedder. Incorrectly referred to by some growers as 'Rufus the Red'.
Nelson – American – 1952

F. simplicicaulis
Tube purplish red, sepals red; corolla purplish red. Flowers are long, borne in clusters at the end of dropping shoots. Long, linear, lanceolate leaves. Tall upright shrub reaching 4–5 m (12–15 ft) in native Peru. Suitable as greenhouse climber.
Ruiz and Pavón – Peru – 1802

'SNOWCAP'
Semi-double. The tube and sepals are bright red with a pure white corolla, slightly veined cerise and although the flowers are smallish in size, it is a most profuse bloomer and considered one of the most free-flowering cultivars in cultivation. Growth is both vigorous and upright and apart from making an exceptionally good bush specimen, can equally be trained as a standard. Easy to grow, is definitely hardy.
Henderson – British – Date unknown

'SOPHISTICATED LADY'
Double. Pale pink tube, sepals very long, pale pink; corolla white. Large blooms, free, very full, with shorter corolla than 'Angel's Flight', but better habit. Growth, a lax bush. Good for baskets.
Martin – American – 1964

'SUSAN TRAVIS'
Single. Tube and slightly recurving sepals, deepish pink; corolla rose pink, paling towards base. Medium-sized flowers, prolific, unusual and welcome break in colour for a hardy. Growth vigorous and spreading, forming a bush

up to 75 cm (2½ ft), hardy.
Travis – British – 1958

'SWINGTIME'
Double. This delightful cultivar is a full double, the short tube and sepals are a rich, shiny red of crepe texture, the inside of the petals being rosy red. The very full corolla is milky, but sparkling white, faintly veined pink. The growth is upright, vigorous and self-branching, responds well to frequent pinching and can be made to trail if necessary; it will, in fact, make a good basket and an exceptionally fine half-basket, although rather on the stiff side. 'Swingtime' is very suitable as an outside bedder and holds its colour extremely well during all

(Above) *'Joy Patmore', very shapely flowers on a vigorous upright plant.*
(Opposite) *'Look East', a fine introduction from Englishman Paul Heavens, is unusual in shape but a delightful colour.*

weathers. Has proved to be hardy. Makes a very fine espalier with careful training and produces a stately standard. 'Titanic' × 'Yuletide'. Tiret – American – 1950

'TAMWORTH'
Single. Tube and sepals crisp, pure white, tipped green, sepals curl out to stem; corolla rich purple at outer edge, changing to band of salmon pink then to white near tube. Light green foliage.

Growth upright and bushy, easy to shape, produces a good bedder for summer display.
Handley – British – 1976

'THALIA'
Triphylla single. Probably the most popular of *F. triphylla* hybrids. 'Thalia' is a German introduction raised by Bonstedt in 1905. Very long tube with tiny sepals and small corolla, the colouring is a self, rich orange-scarlet. The long flowers are borne in profusion in terminal racemes, while the most attractive foliage is a dark olive green, the ribs and veins being of a pronounced magenta. The habit of 'Thalia' is vigorous, usually grown as an upright bush and apart from producing fine specimen plants under glass, is used very extensively for summer bedding. *F. triphylla* ×.
Bonstedt – German – 1905

'TOM THUMB'
Single. Tube and sepals carmine; corolla mauve, veined carmine. Very small flowers, very free, blooms are apt to fall rather prematurely, but owing to profusion hardly noticed. Growth upright, bushy and dwarf, hardy and suitable for rockeries.
Baudinat – French – 1850

'TOM WEST'
Single. Tube and sepals red, corolla purple. Small flowers, not very free and late, grown more for its variegated foliage of cream and pale green. Lax bush or trailer. Possibly a mutation from *riccartonii*.
Miellez – French – 1853

'TRASE'
Semi-double to double. Tube and sepals, carmine-cerise; corolla white veined and flushed carmine-cerise. Medium-sized blooms, very free, excellent shape. Growth upright bushy and hardy; height 45 cm (18 in). One of the best hardies and very suitable as specimen bush plant.
Dawson – British – 1959

'TWINKLING STARS'
Single. Short, thick tube, blush pink, narrow sharply pointed sepals, blush pink outside, pale pink inside. Corolla fuchsia pink. Small flowers held nearly upright, short, even petals, curved tube gives nodding appearance. Early and free flowering. Small foliage growth upright and bushy, very compact, short-jointed.
Handley – British – 1976

'WALSINGHAM'
Semi-double. Off-white tube; sepals off-white outside, rose pink inside and held horizontal. Corolla pale lilac, tight bell shape with crimped edge. Foliage is emerald green, leaves long, pointed and serrated. Growth lax upright and self-branching. Makes magnificent basket. 'Northumbrian Belle' × 'Blush O' Dawn'.
Clitheroe – British – 1979

'WESTMINSTER CHIMES'
Semi-double. Deep rose tube; rose sepals fade to pale pink spreading but not reflexed, tipped green. Corolla violet-blue, ageing to magenta pink at base of petals. Smallish flowers, very profuse. Produces fine hanging pot or

miniature standard. Cascades naturally with lax habit of growth. 'La Campanella' × 'Liebriez'.
Clyne – British – 1976

'WHITE JOY'
Single. Short tube and broadish sepals held horizontally are white with slight pink flush. White corolla, medium-sized flowers perfectly shaped with bell-shaped corolla. Attractive green foliage, growth upright and bushy with short-jointed stems. Will make exceptionally good bush or shrub, also standard and half-hardy bedder. 'Joy Patmore' × 'Eden Lady'.
Burns – British – 1980

'WHITEKNIGHT'S BLUSH'
Single. Pale pink tube, spreading sepals are pale pink with small green tips and lanceolate shaped. Corolla clear pink. The colour of the flowers is similar to *F.*
magellanica var. *molinae* but much larger. Small, dark green foliage. Growth small upright, self-branching, will make good bush and ground cover. Hardy; will make hedge up to 90 cm (3 ft) and take full sun.
Wright (J.) – British – 1980

'WHITEKNIGHT'S PEARL'
Single. Thin white tube; spreading sepals are pale pink with small green tips and lanceolate shaped. Tubular corolla is clear pink with roundish petals. Colour of flowers is similar to *F. magellanica* var. *molinae* but much larger. Small, dark green foliage with no red on veins or branches. Growth medium upright, will make good bush. Hardy, will take full sun and will make hedge up to 1.5 m (5 ft). *F. magellanica* var. *molinae* × (*F. magellanica* var. *molinae* × *F. fulgens*).
Wright. J. – British – 1980

CHAPTER FOUR

GENERAL CULTIVATION

There are three methods of growing fuchsias: current growth, normal growth with pruning and repotting, and also the more advanced method of biennial cultivation. The last is far superior, used by exhibitors to produce their large specimen plants, so I would like to describe this method in general terms before dealing in detail with soil and feeding requirements, growing conditions and general fuchsia care.

Biennial plants are those that complete their flowering in their second year. The start is made by taking cuttings in the early months of the summer, when choice material should be available. When rooted, normally after 14 to 18 days, pot the cuttings singly into 6 cm (2¼ in) pots.

No heat is necessary at this time of year – the plants are left to grow naturally, just feeding, stopping and potting on 2 cm or 1 in at a time. Grow as hard as possible by standing out in the open, or in a cold frame during the whole summer, the objective being to establish a strong, sturdy framework to work upon the following spring. The plants, however, should not be allowed to flower; this is important and is achieved and controlled by regular stopping and pinching out. By early or mid-autumn the plants will be growing either in 10 cm (4 in) or at most 13 cm (5 in) pots. Encourage the plants now to go into a somewhat semi-dormant state, by gradually withholding moisture and feeding. The object during the period of late autumn to midwinter is for the plants just to 'tick over' in green leaf. Here comes the first disadvantage: the temperature needed is 7°C (45°F) allowing for a possible drop to 4°C (40°F), not only during the daytime, but all through the hours of darkness. The plants are not allowed to defoliate as with normal winter care, although it will be natural for a few of the bottom leaves to drop. Careful watering will be required to obtain the ideal soil condition, being one of slight dampness, enough to maintain the foliage in a turgid condition. The plants are really in a state of 'limbo', neither dormant or entirely active, best described as resting.

With the improved light around late winter the plants will take on a completely different look and be ready to be potted back (repotted); those in 13 cm (5 in) pots back to 10 cm (4 in), while those in 10 cm (4 in) pots should be potted back to either 8 cm (3 in) or 9 cm (3½ in). With the biennial plants plenty of new white roots will be evident, unlike normally overwintered plants, but careful handling when potting back will ensure not too many new roots are lost or damaged. There is an alternative method, that of potting on by 2 cm (1 in) larger in late winter, but from experience, the potting back is more successful.

The plants, after either repotting or potting on, are then treated as with any other normal cultivation, with the usual spring and early summer potting programme. Normal feeding programme commences immediately the plant has recovered from any check, concentrating upon a high nitrogenous fertilizer with a 3–1–1 ratio.

Shapes other than the bush or shrub, such as standards, trailers and especially those for baskets, can be grown by the biennial method. The best type of cultivar to select is the strong, upright vigorous cultivar, especially the singles, such as 'Cambridge Louie', 'Countess of Aberdeen' or 'Border Queen'. Probably the biggest disadvantage with growing by the biennial method is that plants grow extremely large and you may have to restrict your number of plants.

TEMPERATURE

Why is it temperatures mean so much? The type of plants we grow most in greenhouses are those killed by frost. Plants hit by frost finish with leaves going limp which soon turn black. The damage is caused by crystals of ice forming inside the plants' cells, making the cell walls distort; when the ice melts, the cells collapse, leaving the plant drooping and glassy looking. On the other hand, too much heat can break down the proteins in a plant, deactivating them; plants lose a lot of water when it is hot. If the water is not replaced because the soil is dry, or if the leaves are losing water faster than the roots can replace it, the plant will wilt. This is because the contents of its cells have lost so much water that they shrink, so the leaves go limp. However, everything gets restored to normal when the temperature drops, so long as the plant has water. Should the plant be left dry after it has wilted, then things can be much more serious. The cell contents shrink so much they actually tear away from the inside of the cell wall. Plants wilt just the same, but will not recover whatever you do.

Most plants have a temperature band in which they live and grow successfully. Just about all expect a difference between day and night temperatures, even though for some it must only be slight.

It is possible to work out reasonable upper and lower temperature limits for a greenhouse, and set automatic vents to operate at the top limit, and the heating to come on at the lower one. A min./max. thermometer is therefore essential for the greenhouse, but it is important where it is placed. Hanging in a sunny position will produce very funny readings, equally it will not be accurate if placed too close to the glass, just above a heater, or just inside a ventila-

tor. The best place is somewhere where the air around it is representative of the air in the whole of the greenhouse, preferably in the shade, at the same height as the plants.

Hardy fuchsias will withstand frost provided their roots are protected by fairly deep planting, but whether hardy or not, any container-planted fuchsias left outside are vulnerable to frost, which will penetrate the container walls. 1°C (33 or 34°F) is sufficient to keep fuchsias frost free during the winter months under cover of a greenhouse or other structure.

During the rest of the year they appreciate an equable temperature without too much day and night variation. The ideal fuchsia temperature for the summer months would be a pleasant and tolerable 15–21°C (60–70°F). While accepting higher temperatures, fuchsias refuse to grow above 24°C (77°F) and we have to make arrangements for heat reduction by shading and ventilation. We can only control temperatures outside by placing plants in shade, which they appreciate.

VENTILATION

When fuchsias are grown under glass, ventilation is just as important an aspect of cultivation as any other. Many growers have been guilty of coddling their fuchsias. *F. magellanica*, from which many of our modern cultivars were bred, was found at the southern extremity of Chile around the Straits of Magellan and has proved the fuchsia is far hardier than originally believed.

As much air as possible should be provided when grown under glass, provided there is no draught. Should you forget to open the ventilators on a hot sunny morning, never rush into the hot house, panic and open all the ventilators and leave the doors wide open. Ventilation should always be carried out in easy stages.

The modern small greenhouse, to cut costs, is usually sold with only one top ventilator. The result is that, when opened, the heavier cold air entering the house sinks down, pushing the lighter warm air through the small ventilator. Unless it is a very warm day, this results in the creation of a cold draught, causing damage to plants. Ventilators should be situated in the roof, at stage level and, if possible, at ground level, in addition to doors at both ends. The opening sequence should be the roof vents first, these will remove the stale air and allow a slow circulation; next the stage vents, to allow a current of air to pass up the glass from the eaves to the ridge. This will cool down the house and at the same time dry up any condensation on the glass (used mainly in hot weather to cool down the greenhouse). However, as fuchsias love a humid, moist atmosphere coupled with fresh air, all ventilators should be opened with great discretion. Finally, the floor vents should be used very sparingly; these are opened to allow a current of air to circulate freely around the actual plants. The doors will allow air to pass right through the house, but the opening of doors other than on very hot days with little wind should be closely watch-

ed as all humidity can be lost with doors wide open. Ventilation should be given early in the day, in order that the house has time to build up a reasonable temperature again after ventilation and before the air outside drops in temperature. This period will obviously vary according to the season.

Now, having said all this, as far as my own fuchsias are concerned, they are grown as hard as possible, which means that by late spring, unless gales and high winds are around, my top vents are left open at all times until mid-autumn. The stage ventilators are then used with care – the days have to be very warm before they are fully opened. You may consider the fitting of louvres in the greenhouse sides; often with strong breezes blowing, it is handy to be able to adjust the opening to prevent direct draughts.

How do you provide ventilation during your absence? The automatic vent opener is the answer. These units ensure that some ventilation is provided when there is a sudden rise in temperature. These openers are operated by a heat-sensitive component, so there is no need for any electrical supply. The opener usually starts to operate at 15°C (60°F) but can be adjusted. They are usually fitted to the roof ventilators but can be used for side vents, each unit lifting about 7 kg (15 lb).

An exchange of air inside the greenhouse encourages better growth and prevents stagnant air, the cause of some

'Orange Drops' remains our best orange. Lax in habit with its flowers hanging in clusters.

plant diseases. Electric fans, or the fan of a greenhouse heater will move the air well. Extractor fans ensure a good exchange of air, ideally about 20 to 30 changes per hour. A sliding door is also much better than the conventional door for keeping internal temperatures and humidity right. It can be used as a large ventilator and easily adjusted as required.

SHADING

The fuchsia in its natural environment grows mainly in the dappled shade of the rain forests or the mountain slopes. In this country we grow it somewhat artificially, especially when under glass, and must therefore provide adequate shading during the summer months.

Lath blinds are ideal for imitating that dappled shade; they are, however, very expensive. Green polythene blinds fitted inside are acceptable but play havoc with colour renderings. Several types of plastic mesh give excellent results.

When using mesh never lay it flat on the glass – always leave at least 2.5 cm (1 in) between the glass and the mesh, otherwise you will increase the heat instead of lowering it.

Probably from the cost point of view, most of us resort to providing shade by coating the glass with a temporary 'paint'. White is the best colour as it reflects back more heat. The cheapest and easiest method is to mix ordinary plain flour or whitening with water, adding a little salt to aid adhesion. Decorator's size is even better, but use in moderation, or it may be difficult to

remove in the autumn. The best type of shading paint is a product called Varishade, a non-toxic substance developed by Solar Sunstill USA, but readily available elsewhere. It shades out excessive solar light and heat when dry, yet when wet with rain becomes practically transparent; when the coating dries it again becomes opaque. Another advantage is that when it is applied to the inside of the glass, the normal condensation, which can often remain up to 10 a.m., will keep the shading transparent. This is particularly useful during spring, early summer and autumn. The product can be sprayed or brushed on, although my personal choice is the decorator's roller. It is easily removed by washing down when the season is finished; the manufacturers claim that if so desired it will last three years. My second choice would be Coolglass, which mixes instantly with cold water and is easily applied by brush or spray. It is removable with the flick of a duster, yet is absolutely fast in rain, harmless to plants and will not contaminate collected rainwater.

Where fuchsias are concerned early shading is advisable. I apply a thin coat of it in early to mid spring, then when plants are more mature, especially in bud or flower, I give an extra coat to prolong their life.

WATERING

When growing in the wild fuchsias receive an annual rainfall of between 500 cm and 750 cm (200–300 in) and like to be moist but never waterlogged.

Watering under glass is an important aspect of cultivation – master the watering can and 75% of greenhouse management is solved. Watering outside in the border is not so critical except during hot spells.

Rain or tap? It is a mistake to equate rainwater to distilled water: it is not sterile, but contains carbon from atmospheric soot, various trace gases and wind-borne dust particles and can, at times, be contaminated with extra radio-activity. The real difference is in the higher calcium content of tap water. This is acquired by the rain falling on limestone before it filters into streams and so reaches the reservoirs. The deposit it leaves in your kettles – and those white markings left on your fuchsia foliage after you have sprayed – separate tap water from rainwater. Use hard tap water on potted azaleas and just watch them lose colour and life. Most of us try to collect as much rainwater as possible. The catchment area should be as large as possible; any roof is acceptable provided it is not dirty; gutterings, therefore, must be kept clean. For small needs the greenhouse roof could yield enough, but the water needs to be filtered to remove all particles of grime and leaves, with a fine-mesh filter. The maxim with any water should be 'If you can't drink it, then don't use it.' I must admit that with a very large greenhouse, through necessity, I use my mains water, which is hard whether it contains excessive lime or not. In fact, fuchsias tolerate lime, although do not particularly like it.

The old method of testing whether plants needed watering was to tap the pot – clay pots produce a distinct ringing sound should the compost be dry, or a dull dead one if it is moist. Now that plastic pots are almost universally used in conjunction with soilless composts, this method is useless (plastic pots will always produce a dead sound). The only sure method to judge the moisture content is by weight. In a very short period, experience will tell you when you pick up a pot whether it feels heavy or light: if heavy, leave it alone; if light, water it well; if in doubt, leave it until next time. When watering, really soak the compost. Then leave alone until just before the plant needs watering again, then give another good soaking. It is not generally realized that the plants' growing potential is at the maximum just before they need water. Never give little dribbles every day – that is the quickest way to kill any plant. Always water from the top; provided your drainage is correct, the plant will absorb all the water it requires. If you water from the bottom, how do you know just how much to give? The plant could stand with its feet in water for some period, so the soil becomes waterlogged, the roots cannot breathe and in some cases plants just die through suffocation of the root system. If you must use saucers, make certain you drain away any surplus water after watering.

During very warm spells I may use the hosepipe for damping down purposes to create humidity, but not to water the plants. First, the pressure is too great unless some kind of filter or siphon is employed, and secondly, water coming direct from the mains supply is too cold and likely to check growth. All plants should be handled and treated individually. It is thoroughly bad gardening husbandry to treat and water a whole batch of plants exactly the same, just because the first one or two tested needed watering. Always try to finish your watering by early afternoon; unless absolutely necessary plants should never be watered at night. The reason that it is a very bad practice is because you are adding to the moisture always present in the night air, which cannot be absorbed. This will cause damping-off of flowers and the premature dropping of buds.

Overhead spraying with a fine mist is beneficial in keeping down the temperature and the damp atmosphere so created discourages pests, particularly the red spider. Spraying should not, however, be done during any cold weather as this would encourage botrytis. Spraying can be continued right up to bud and flower stage, then discontinued as moisture on flowers will cause spotting and brown marking, particularly on the pale-coloured and white cultivars.

Fuchsias dislike high temperatures and a danger during very hot spells is over-watering, which is often fatal. In hot weather do not in any circumstances add more water to a pot or basket that already has moist compost, even if the plants are limp with wilted foliage. Lightly spray the foliage first, place in a shaded position and wait to see if the plant picks up. If it doesn't, start checking for poor drainage or over-watering. Under such conditions is the time when I prefer clay pots with a soil-based compost; the extra thickness of the clay protects the roots better and helps them to breathe. Do not leave plants in plastic pots in the midday sun; the excessive heat will penetrate the thin wall and burn up the delicate hairy roots.

Fuchsias in pots or containers outside on the patio and elsewhere will need watering regularly, even when it is actually raining; it takes at least four hours of continuous rain to give the compost the same moisture content as obtainable from the watering can.

Plants in the border for the summer display will rarely need any watering except during heat waves, if they are planted directly into the ground. Those plants bedded out as half-hardies in their own pots, plunged in the ground to pot level, will need constant watering, which is best done with the hosepipe. Hardy plants in the border during their first summer will also need constant attention and must never want for moisture until they are firmly established, which may be the following year.

FEEDING and FERTILIZERS

Human beings feed to live but without a regular supply of starch, protein and minerals would soon die. Plants, however, are different – as long as certain chemicals are available to their root system, they are able to make their own starch, protein and the rest. It is the

(Opposite) *A recent breakthrough, 'Our Ted' is the long sought white triphylla raised by Edwin Goulding.*

minute root-hairs just behind the tip of the root that form the 'mouth' of the plant. Fuchsias are heavy feeders; they must be fed, especially when established and in flower, or they will produce fewer and smaller blooms of poorer colour. Continuous balanced feeding will prolong flowering even into mid- or late autumn – until the first frosts or bad light, whichever is the sooner.

Feeding can commence in a weak form as soon as young plants have established themselves in their first pot, then continued throughout the life of the plant. A wise policy would be to standardize upon a certain, calculated strength of fertilizer at the commencement of the season and then to increase the frequency instead of increasing the strength. This manner of application is a more balanced programme and allows for feeding at every watering, but with the emphasis very much upon a weak feed.

Never feed plants when dry at the roots, this results in the burning up of the small hairy roots. Never feed sickly looking plants. Although fuchsias are a glutton for their feed, they can be overfed, which causes lush growth, especially if over-potted at the same time. This condition will produce leaf at the expense of flower and the plant will be more prone to pests and diseases. Always read the instructions on the label and never apply at more than the stated strength.

Fertilizers are classfied into two categories: organic and inorganic. The former are obtained from animal or vegetable origin, while the latter are artificial and manufactured. Both are known as major plant foods and contain three elements: nitrogen, phosphorus and potassium (generally called nitrogen, phosphates and potash and referred to as N–P–K). Before using any fertilizers we should know what they contain and what specific purposes the elements perform.

NITROGEN (N)

A most essential element as it stimulates the growth of healthy green leaves, as well as the growth of the stem and laterals and increases the size of the plant. Bonemeal, hoof and horn meal and dried blood are organic substances supplying nitrogen, whereas chemicals such as sulphate of ammonia and nitrate of soda both give a rapid release of nitrogen. A shortage of nitrogen is indicated in plants which are stunted with small, pale leaves.

PHOSPHATES (P)

This element stimulates the growth of the root system and speeds up flowering or fruiting. Shortages are indicated by signs of stunted plants with poorly developed roots. Superphosphate of lime is a quick-acting inorganic fertilizer and bonemeal is slow-acting and organic.

POTASH (K)

The symbol for potassium, 'K', may be confusing and is derived from the Latin word *kalium*. This is most essential for plants, for without it they cannot make full use of the nitrogen for leaf and stem growth. It helps to prevent soft growth, improves the colour of the flower and increases resistance to diseases. A deficiency is indicated in the scorching of the leaves at the edges, poorly coloured flowers lacking in size and quantity. An inorganic source is sulphate of potash, quick-acting with a high concentration. Wood ashes are organic, but with a low concentration – down to 1.7% unless stored under cover.

All proprietary fertilizers contain these three major elements and the numbers quoted on the label are used to indicate the strength of each element: 9–6–4, for example, would indicate the percentage of nitrogen, phosphates and potash, in that order – 9%N 6%P 4%K. The content varies from brand to brand but the NPK ratio must by law in UK and USA be quoted on the label.

Having ascertained which specific purpose each element performs, a balanced feeding programme for the season can be recommended. In the early stages of growth up to early/midsummer, a fertilizer with a high content of nitrogen is used, with a ratio around 3–1–1.

From bud and flower stage a switch is made to a high content of potash ratio 1–1–3. There is a short period of about two weeks just before and immediately at bud stage, where a balanced 1–1–1 ratio fertilizer is beneficial.

□ TRACE ELEMENTS

Trace elements are essential for good cultivation, and usually a large reserve is found in all good composts. One very important one is magnesium (Mg) and when plants are grown in the same compost for more than one season, the supply of magnesium becomes exhausted, especially where plants are not repotted. The shortage is indicated by leaves having yellow streaks and spots, the lower leaves eventually dropping off. If not corrected, general yellowing of the foliage follows and decay sets in. The remedy is simple: a tablespoon of magnesium sulphate (Epsom salts) to the gallon of water (20ml per 5 litres), applied two or three times at weekly intervals at the first indication of trouble. Another cause for the yellowing of the leaves, this time the upper leaves, is a deficiency of iron. The remedy can be effected with two or three applications of sulphate of iron (ferrous sulphate), also at the rate of one tablespoon to the gallon (20ml per 5 litres).

□ ORGANIC FERTILIZERS

Some growers believe that various animal manures contain high food value; they are, in fact, very low in NPK value. An analysis of one ton of good decayed stable manure contains approximately 0.5% nitrogen, 0.35% phosphates, 0.5% potash and 0.7% lime. All the rest is either moisture or humus matter, which is of value but not nutritive.

□ SLOW-RELEASE FERTILIZERS

These comparatively new fertilizers are now widely used, especially by nurserymen, as they save both time and energy. The rate of fertilizer released is governed by the soil temperature and is only operative around 21°C (70°F). The obvious advantage is that one application will last for the whole growing

season. The two most popular feeds are Osmocote (NPK) 18–11–10, a coated granular fertilizer which is released over six to nine months, and Osmocote 14–14–14, the best for fuchsias, which has a controlled short-term release of three to four months.

Finally there is one fertilizer which I refer to as a 'dark secret' – very rarely used but most effective, cheap although not always easy to obtain – SOOT. This is a straight fertilizer containing only a small proportion of nitrogen, varying from 1% to 7%, but it does contain an amount of sulphur and a useful supply of trace elements. It must be stored and weathered under cover for at least three months, the light fluffy soot being better than the heavier dense types. It is watered down to the colour of weak tea by immersion and applied twice a week in addition to normal feeding. This will impart a sheen to the foliage and improve the colour of the flowers to an almost unbelievable extent.

POTTING COMPOSTS

The medium in which plants are cultivated is all important – without the right material, our skills are wasted. Should the question be asked, 'What is the ideal potting compost?' I would immediately reply, 'John Innes No.2 soil-based compost with plants grown in clay pots'. The difficulty, however, is in obtaining a good compost to the John Innes formula, as very inferior composts are sold

'Pink Marshmallow' is a large double white with pink overtones, fine for baskets.

today, with almost anything acting as a substitute for the all-important loam. However, there is an alternative which is now used universally and produces excellent results: soilless compost. But let us first study the actual ingredients that contribute to all potting composts.

SOIL
Soil is the top 10–45 cm (4–18 in) or so of the earth's surface on which plant life grows (lacking, as has been discovered, on the surface of the Moon or Mars!). Formed from pulverized rock, decayed vegetation, decomposed plants and animal remains, it is the body of all soils and composts.

All soils have what is known as a pH factor, which refers to the relative acidity or alkalinity in the soil. The pH factor of 7 indicates neutrality, any figure lower than that, as far as 3.5, indicates increasing acidity, while figures between 7 and 9.5 show the relative alkalinity of the soil.

The scale of 3.5 to 9.5 is logarithmic, which means that pH5 is ten times as much as pH6, and pH4 is 100 times as much as pH6. All intermediate values are expressed as decimals.

The ideal pH factor for fuchsias is 6.8, which is slightly acid. They do not particularly like lime but will tolerate it reasonably well.

LOAM
Loam is obtained from rotted turves taken from the top 10–15 cm (4–6 in) of rich pasture which has yielded a good growth of grass. The original John Innes formula required 'a good medium loam, slightly greasy when smeared without

being sticky' – a tight specification, but one which indicates the right clay content. Turves are stacked up to twelve months, grass side down and, when rotted, turn into fibrous loam. After sterilization the loam should have a pH factor of 6.5 to 6.8.

PEAT

The ideal peat is sphagnum – fibrous, soft and moisture-absorbent, it allows easy passage of air throughout the mixture. It will hold up to 15 times its own weight of water, is rather acid with a pH figure of approximately 4.5. Sedge peat on the other hand, being made up of sedges, reeds, mosses and trees, is very hard, unkind to the 'touch', difficult to wet, yet stubborn to yield moisture. Once dry it is difficult to wet again, it holds only seven to eight times its own weight of water, and has a pH factor which can vary between 3.5 and 7.0.

SAND

The ideal sand is washed sand, graded evenly up to 3 mm (⅛in) – fine sands should be avoided. Sand as a compost ingredient is now largely replaced by 4 mm washed grit. Washed Cornish sea sand is ideal, but on no account should either builders' sand or untreated sea sand be used; both are too fine and contain injurious salts. Any sand or grit used *must* be washed.

PERLITE

This material, now widely used, consists of inert, sponge-like glassy granules of volcanic origin. It is expanded by intensive heat treatment which gives a microscopic internal cell structure. Per-

lite improves aeration, drainage and water retention in soils and composts, and generally speaking can be used in place of sand or grit.

VERMICULITE

Vermiculite is an ultra-lightweight sterile material holding many times its own weight in water, which it releases when needed. Vermiculite is made from laminated mica, a mineral, subjected to high temperatures which expand it into concertina-like granules containing thousands of open cells. It is now being used to improve composts.

Composts are the balanced mixtures of various potting ingredients mixed to promote the cultivation of plants grown in pots and containers and as such should: (a) retain moisture (i.e. contain peat or perlite); (b) although moisture-retaining, be well-drained (i.e. contain sand or grit); (c) contain humus, the body of the mixture, but not be too loose (i.e. loam); (d) contain the necessary food or nutrients (i.e. fertilizers)

□ SOIL-BASED COMPOSTS

The main soil-based composts consist of the following ingredients which are always measured by bulk and not by weight:

SEED	2 parts loam, 1 part peat and 1 part sand.
CUTTING	1 part loam, 2 parts peat and 1 part sand.
POTTING	7 parts loam, 3 parts peat and 2 parts sand.

Prior to the 1930s all composts were mixed to individual requirements. It was not until Lawrence and Newell had carried out years of experimentation at the John Innes Institute that they eventually recommended their famous formula for the cultivation of plants grown in pots and containers.

Should a potting compost be required to the John Innes formula then to each bushel (36 litres) of potting ratio (7 parts loam, 3 parts peat and 2 parts sand) is added 112 g (4 oz) of John Innes base fertilizer which is made up of:

2 parts hoof and horn 3 mm (⅛ in) grist
2 parts superphosphate of lime
1 part sulphate of potash

to which 21 g (¾ oz) of limestone or chalk is added. The analysis of this fertilizer is 5.1% nitrogen, 7.2% phosphates and 9.7% potash. The various strengths of John Innes potting composts are known as No.1, No.2 and No.3 which may be confusing to the uninitiated and simply relate to the amount of base fertilizer added to each bushel. No.1 contains 112 g (4 oz), No. 2 double the amount, while No.3 contains 336 g (12 oz).

For the potting of fuchsias No.1 is used for potting up to and including 10 cm (4 in); No.2 for pots 10–15 cm (4–6 in) and No.3 for the final potting into larger containers.

The test for ascertaining the correct moisture content of any soil-based compost is to grip a handful of the compost. On release it should stay firm momentarily, then begin to crumble.

When any soil-based compost is mixed with a base fertilizer, it should be used within eight weeks of mixing. After that period the toxic salts accumulating in the compost build up into ammonia, turning the compost sour.

Sources of good John Innes composts made up to the correct formula and using the right ingredients are now increasingly difficult to locate. Fortunately, several manufacturers have recently joined forces to form the John Innes Manufacturers' Association, to control the standard of composts produced by their members and guaranteeing the use of specific ingredients. Details are obtainable from J.I.M.A. Horticultural Trades Association, Reading, Berks RG3 2DE.

Provided a good loam can be located, my formula for an excellent soil-based compost for fuchsias, provided no objection is made to unsterilized loam, would be 2 parts unsterilized loam, 1 part sphagnum peat and 1 part coarse sand or 4 mm grit to which 112 g (4 oz) of J.I. base fertilizer without chalk is added to each bushel (36 litres). As an alternative to the J. I. base fertilizer, use 112 g (4 oz) of Vitax Q4 or Chempak Potting Base.

☐ SOILLESS COMPOSTS

An alternative for potting plants, almost universally used, are the soilless composts marketed under various proprietary brand names, all of which are suitable for fuchsia cultivation. Most of these brand composts are made, with certain modifications, to the 'D' mix which originated in the University of California many years ago. The specification of the 'D' mix is 75% sphagnum

'Pride of the West' is one of the few cultivars suitable for training as a climber.

peat with 25% washed silicate quartz sand and certain fertilizers added. Some growers, however, find that some brands, although quite excellent composts, are very loose in texture and extremely light in weight. This can result in plants with even average top growth becoming top heavy, which makes staking a problem. Over the years, I have been completely satisfied with the Humber soilless compost (obtainable from Humber Manures Ltd of Stoneferry, Hull, who will advise of their nearest stockists). A major advantage is the inclusion of heavy sand and grit providing instant drainage whilst supporting canes up to 1.5m (5ft). It also reduces watering with its moisture-retaining qualities, and promotes a better rooting system.

REPOTTING

Repotting is often confused with potting on and is exactly the opposite operation. Repotting means potting *back*, usually into a smaller container. The timing depends upon the condition of the plant, coupled with weather conditions and the amount of heat available. Any plant which has flowered the previous summer needs repotting after pruning, when the first pair of leaves appear.

'Roy Walker' is probably the best of the very upright-growing double whites.

The plant should be slightly on the dry side, with as much of the old soil removed as possible. Try not to damage any new roots, distinguishable by being white as opposed to the old, expanded brown roots. Any damaged or excessive root growth can be pruned to advantage, but be careful with an older plant's tap root, which can bleed. Some growers will even wash away all traces of soil under the tap.

Plant back into a clean pot just slightly larger than the ball of roots and vestiges of old soil. Use fresh compost. Never use old compost or leave plants growing on in the same compost which has lost nutrients, especially the trace elements. The leaves of starved plants will turn yellow, particularly between the veins, and eventually brown. Another reason for repotting is the chance to check for the vine weevil grubs, which can eat away entire root systems. Often it is possible to repot from 15cm (6in) to 10cm (4in) or from 13cm (5)in) to 9cm (3½in). It is stressed you will not produce a plant of any quality without the essential operations of both pruning and repotting.

When the newly formed roots are moving nicely around the outside of the rootball, without getting in any way pot bound, the plant can be potted on into

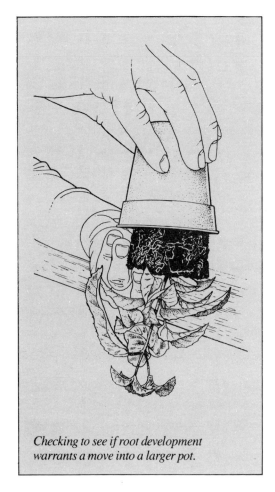

Checking to see if root development warrants a move into a larger pot.

its next size pot in the normal manner. Repotting should be carried out as necessary throughout the plant's lifetime. With some established plants of considerable age and in large pots, it may be necessary, after removing the old soil, to move back into the same pot. If this is not possible, remove as much as possible of the old soil at the base, possibly 5 cm (2 in) and also the top 5 cm (2 in), replacing it with new compost.

Large specimens, especially standards and plants in tubs or large pots, particularly require this treatment. Finger pressure is all that is needed for most plants. Those in large pots need much firmer pressure but without resorting to the rammer.

WINTER CARE

When overwintering fuchsias, two important factors must always be in mind: plants must be frost-free and they must never be allowed to dry out.

As autumn approaches, the ripening of the wood is the first stage of the preparation of plants for their winter rest. If plants are not already outside they should be exposing their growth by late summer, for the maturing and gradual ripening of the wood. Plants will withstand the vigours of the oncoming winter better with ripe wood than with young, green, sappy growth. At this time you would normally have stopped feeding, but two or three applications of a high potash fertilizer, such as sulphate of potash (48.8%K) or Phostrogen (26.5%K) will assist in hardening off. Another method of ripening the wood on plants which have stayed in the greenhouse, is to leave all the ventilators and doors wide open on suitable occasions, until the first frosts.

Early autumn will also be the time to be selective about those plants to be carried on by overwintering, discarding all that did not come up to expectations. Gradually withhold water, thus encouraging the loss of yellowing bottom leaves. Forget about all autumn pruning

Preparing to bury fuchsias in peat under the greenhouse staging for the winter.

– leave that for the very early spring. You can, however, carry out shaping by trimming back and removing one-third of the growth made during the summer.

When plants are brought back into the greenhouse or conservatory, aim to keep the temperature no lower than 4°C (40°F) especially for species, *triphyllas* and standards. Whips (young, unstopped plants) together with plants being trained as standards, espaliers and similar shapes, together with any autumn-struck cuttings, need to be kept in green leaf, just ticking over. Those plants growing on the biennial method need a temperature around 7°C (45°F). By late autumn the remaining plants will show definite signs of requiring their winter rest and if they have not shed their foliage, remove all leaves, leaving just bare stems and framework. Although a

temperature of 4°C (40°F) should try to be maintained, you can safely overwinter plants by keeping them slightly moist in a temperature just above freezing point. They will even stand a degree or two of frost, provided it is not of any long duration.

Should you not possess any artificial heat, it is still possible to overwinter successfully and simply. This time, having gone through the routine of shaping the plants and taking off the foliage, it matters little where you store them. The greenhouse is the obvious place, but the cold frame, garage, shed or even the spare bedroom are suitable, provided they are frost-free. One method I use successfully is storing the plants under the greenhouse staging. Lay them in their pots side by side, all tall-trained plants, together with standards first, followed by the smaller bush/shrub types. All are packed together as close as possible, one on top of the other, laying horizontally. The whole lot is then completely covered with sphagnum peat, neither dry nor wet but just nicely moist. Stems, together with the whole pot, supports and labels are completely covered, leaving no trace of the plants visible. Apart from the occasional check during the winter, to ascertain the condition of the soil in the pot, which should remain moist, the whole lot is left without heat of any description until late winter/early spring. They are then unearthed with the young, fresh, pink eyes already formed, in time for pruning. This method is almost foolproof, provided you do not have the peat too wet; otherwise mildew and botrytis could be a problem. Should the winter be not too severe, wherever you store the plants, covering with sacking, brown paper or even newspaper can save your plants when frosts are forecast – but the winter has to be mild.

The last method is put the plants under the care of Mother Nature by burying in the open ground. Dig a trench some 60 cm (2 ft) deep and 45 cm (18 in) wide, which could be lined with straw or peat. Then, after trimming and shaping and removing canes, place the pots close together on their sides in the trench, and cover with either peat, sand, ashes or leaves. Soil is not favoured, as it encourages pests and worms, while a certain amount of damage can be made to new growth when lifting. Fill the trench, making a mound over the plants, much the same as a clamp of potatoes or dahlia tubers. If the plants are well buried the frosts will not penetrate and will withstand any winter. Lifting will be made in mid-spring ready for cultivation in the new season.

YEAR-ROUND PROGRAMME

□ MIDWINTER
Hardies in the border may need protection of layers of peat at their base and crown. Under glass, when the sun expands the mercury, spray awakening plants in the morning. Plants will benefit from as much light as possible – a good fall of snow works wonders on light reflection. Two killers are botrytis and weevil grubs; watch out for both. Air circulation combined with a little heat will help to combat botrytis.

□ LATE WINTER
Spray plants with luke-warm water to soften the wood and encourage new eyes. Heavy watering, which awakening roots cannot cope with, should be avoided. Time for stock plants to start moving; watch for new growth appearing from below soil level. Pruning should now almost be completed and repotting (potting back) in operation when the first pair of leaves form. Order or purchase your new potting compost, now is the best time to purchase new plants as rooted cuttings.

□ EARLY SPRING
The ideal time for taking cuttings. Concentrate upon the tip cutting which produces superior plants. Shoots will be

appearing everywhere, so provide that little extra heat when nights are cold to maintain growth. When pruning is finished and most repotting completed, some early repots may need their first potting on. Early rooted cuttings will reach their second potting-on stage. Keep the size of the pot down to a minimum. First feeding can commence with very weak nitrogenous fertilizer. Baskets can be planted at the end of the month.

□ MID-SPRING

With growth happening everywhere in the greenhouse now is the time to apply shading. Last chance to set up baskets, preferably use 9 cm (3½ in) pot plants and remember that one type of cultivar produces better results. Space out all plants on the staging – no leaf should overlap another. Potting on should be in full swing. As soon as roots are girdling the rootball or popping out of the bottom of the pot, move the plant into the next-sized pot – but no larger than 2 cm or 1 in at a time. Continue to feed with a nitrogenous fertilizer.

□ LATE SPRING

Provided new growth has appeared at the base of hardy plants in the border, hard pruning down to soil level can be undertaken. Too early yet for the planting of the new hardy cultivars or bedding out as half-hardies. All plants, especially cuttings and young, green growth, must have protection from strong sunlight. Shading is essential now. Extremely busy period: time not long enough for all the potting on,

stopping and pinching, watering and the constant spraying and damping down. Watchful eye is now necessary for pests, especially the first to appear: greenflies. Keep an aerosol containing malathion handy and use at first sign. When spraying, make sure the temperature is reasonably high; sprays are useless in low temperatures. Ideal time for training standards, starting with unstopped rooted cutting in 8 cm (3 in) pot, grown up on single stem.

□ EARLY SUMMER

Last chance for final potting: 13 cm (5 in) size for current growth. All pinching and stopping should now be terminated unless late flowering is required. Plant out in the border both hardies and half-hardies for the summer display. Continue to spray all plants, pots and staging with clear water until bud stage. Physically handle each and every plant at least once a week, checking for moisture and particularly for pests.

□ MIDSUMMER

Make sure outside hardies and half-hardies do not want for moisture, provide adequate staking for the standards and remember to feed. Baskets tend to dry out very quickly, plunge and soak as often as possible. Buds and flowers appear everywhere, continue to feed, switching over to high-potash fertilizer. Any bush/shrub plants needing support should have canes positioned early to allow plants to grow around them; all staking should be unobtrusive. Solid staging is preferred to slatted type as it can be covered with gravel which is kept moist through the summer to keep the air round the plants humid.

☐ LATE SUMMER

Watering now becomes the all-consuming task required practically every day. Carry out operation before mid-day and never at night, water from the top, aim to keep moist, never wet. The task of removing spent seed pods is very necessary if plants are to continue flowering. Potting on for the current season should cease – never pot on plants in full flower. Pruning back plants, particularly those outside, to three or four pairs of leaves will produce admirable cutting material for taking as autumn cuttings. Biennial plants for next year should now be unflowered in 10 cm (4 in) pots and pinched back frequently.

☐ EARLY AUTUMN

Now is the most susceptible time for both whitefly and red spider. Watch out for signs especially on the underside of the foliage. Important that high degree of hygiene be maintained, remove all signs of debris and faded blooms, many plants should be providing second flush of flower. Essential that a high potash feed be maintained, this will assist in the continuation of flower and the early ripening of the wood. Although night temperatures may drop, there is no need to close either doors or ventilators; plants need all the fresh air possible to assist in ripening. Provided you can find shoots without bud or flower, start taking autumn cuttings.

☐ MID-AUTUMN

Remember, no pruning (an early spring operation) but a start can be made on shaping plants by removing one-third of the season's growth. Start can also be made on lifting the half-hardies used for summer bedding. Begin the important task of selecting and discarding plants before overwintering. Cooler nights coupled with evening mists and heavy dews make for fuchsia paradise and easier watering with alternate daily watering. Ripen off the wood by giving plants two or three applications of a very high-potash fertilizer. Remove all shading from greenhouse roof to let in as much light as possible. Make preparation for overwintering. Slight heat may be needed if young plants and cuttings are to remain in leaf.

☐ LATE AUTUMN

Watch the hygiene – dead flowers, foliage and seed pods can cause botrytis. Biennial plants and autumn cuttings need 7°C (45°F). Careful with the watering, just enough to keep the sap alive, except for biennial plants. Remember standards, tall types of training and *triphyllas* need a minimum of 4°C (40°F). Overwintering is now in operation. Start to remove all foliage and shape plants that need resting by removing one-third growth. Do not prune hardies, just shape by removing one-third of growth. Ventilate freely during any mild spell. Any plants left out as half-hardies in beds and plants on the patio must be brought in under cover if you wish to save them for next season or grow them on to yield cuttings.

□ EARLY WINTER

Dull and short days help no plants, so provide as much light as possible. If you must use bubble or plastic linings make sure ventilators are free to open. Watch for any signs of botrytis; damp, cold and stagnant conditions encourage it, buoyant atmosphere and ventilation prevent it. Use benomyl on affected wood. Careful with the watering; soil in pots should be only slightly moist. Very quiet period for fuchsias, if you have to use an insecticide, better to fumigate than spray. After selecting and removing plants for overwintering, the greenhouse should be half-full in preparation for the spring. Remember more plants are killed from lack of moisture by becoming dust dry than from the cold.

PESTS and DISEASES

There is a point of especial merit in favour of the fuchsia: its immunity to most pests and diseases which attack other plants. Even those grown outside in the border suffer little damage. Provided routine hygiene and a regular spraying or fumigation programme is carried out, most pests can be kept at bay. Many potential pests relish dry conditions, so creating the correct environment, with humidity between 45 and 60%, coupled with cleanliness will deter most troubles. When conditions under glass are warm, during the late spring and summer, humidity must be maintained by constant damping down and spraying.

Most pests are located on the underside of leaves, one of the main reasons why plants should be handled physically at least once a week. Do we spray or fumigate? Fumigation is preferable, especially at bud or flower stage as it prevents any marking of blooms. It is also advantageous during the winter, for the prevention of damp atmospheric conditions. Whether spraying or fumigation is carried out it should be done in fairly high temperatures, around 18°C (65°F), preferably in the early evening or during dull, cloudy weather. When using all sprays it is advisable to add a teaspoon of household detergent to the gallon (20 ml to each 5 litres) to assist as a wetting agent. When spraying, plants should never be dry at the roots and it is essential that the wetting of the underside of leaves be thorough to kill all the pests there.

The following list of pests may look rather menacing but in practice, it is most unusual to encounter more than a few in only one garden.

□ ANTS (*Acanthonyops niger* or *Lasius niger*)

No description necessary. Ants can be troublesome by tunnelling and moving soil around both inside and outside the greenhouse. Although doing little damage, they are responsible for the spreading of aphids, transporting them to new plants. Ants feed on sugary plant or pest secretions; winged forms develop in mid- and late summer and fly off to start new colonies. They find dry atmospheric conditions to their liking. Control by dusting or spraying with HCH; also dust infested areas with ant-killer.

Semi-double 'Snowcap', one of the best known fuchsias and in most collections.

APHIDS (many species)

The most common aphid to attack fuchsias, both inside and outside, is the peach-potato aphid (*Myzus persicae*). They can be green, brown, pink, black or red, up to 3mm (⅛in) long; some are winged. Aphids exude honeydew which acts as a medium for sooty mould (*Cladosporium* spp.), an unsightly black fungus. They cluster on stems, particularly young soft shoot tips, causing distortion of shoot and leaf. Their presence is indicated by leaf curl, caused by their sucking out of the sap. Control by spraying with derris, malathion, pyrethrum and dimethoate. Fumigate with HCH, nicotine or malathion aerosol.

BEES

Although not really classified as a pest, bees can do untold damage, especially in the greenhouse while searching for nectar. They will bruise and mark flowers. As bees are daytime visitors they are difficult to control; the only remedy is covering ventilators and doors with suitable mesh or netting.

CAPSID BUG (*Lygocoris pabulinus*)

These small green or brown, fast-moving pests up to 6mm (¼in) long with long legs similar to aphids, will disappear under the leaves at the slightest touch. Leaf cells are pierced, which then die, giving a tattered appearance. It is the young growth which is most attacked, with shoots going blind. You will see leaves punctured with small holes, the sap sucked out causing them to blister and turn red. Capsid bugs mainly attack outdoor fuchsias, but can attack indoors, too. The control is to spray with HCH or malathion, or to fumigate with HCH or gamma HCH.

ELEPHANT HAWK MOTH CATERPILLAR

Young caterpillars are green and brown in colour being both large 8cm (3in) and terribly destructive. They will devour the entire leaves of a plant in a night, before moving on to the next. They can be found both inside and outside, and feed also on honeysuckle, lilac and petunias, their host plant being the willowherb. The only effective control is hand picking, especially at night.

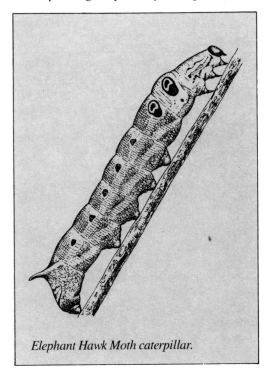

Elephant Hawk Moth caterpillar.

□ FROGHOPPER OR CUCKOOSPIT (*Philaenus spumarius*)

This leaf-sucking pest resembles a miniaturized frog 6mm (¼in) long which leaps when disturbed. The nymphs surround themselves with a blob of froth, under the protection of which they feed like their parents. Known as 'cuckoospit', it is seen in May, about the time the cuckoo returns. This is an outside pest, very rarely seen under glass. The remedy is the complete removal of the spittle, which can be done by spraying with an insecticide, or even a strong spray of water.

□ FUCHSIA MITE (*Aculops fuchsiae*)

This is an extremely serious pest which originated in Brazil and has been threatening the existence of the fuchsia in California. It has been confused with the Western Flower Thrip. It is an eriophyid mite which damages the growing points and the flowers of fuchsias. The early stages look similar to damage from a heavy aphid infestation, with tissues thickened and distorted. Further progression of damage eventually results in plant parts that no longer look like leaves as they become grotesquely malformed, resembling peach leaf curl. The mites are only 0.15mm long, wormlike with only two pairs of legs. An early symptom of the mite is a puckering of young leaves, with the upper surface blistering and hairy, which could be mistaken for an attack of mildew. Control is extremely difficult and little progress has been made to find a remedy.

□ LEAF HOPPER (*Zygina pallidifrons*)

These yellowish insects with vertically held wings are just half the size of the froghopper, hopping when disturbed and found only outside. They breed and feed on the lower surface of leaves, producing tiny yellow flecks or blotches on the leaf tissue. Control is by spraying with malathion, pyrethrum or dimethoate at weekly intervals.

□ RED SPIDER (*Tetranychus urticae* and *T. cinnabarinus*

The worst pest to attack fuchsias, especially under glass, and difficult to detect in early stages, is really a sucking mite and not a spider. Tiny greenish or yellow minute pests less than 0.5mm long, visible only to the naked eye as a kind of rust on the underside of the leaves, they can also be red or brown. The mites cause yellow speckled foliage but in severe attacks the leaves become dry like parchment and covered in fine web. They feed on the underside of leaves and on young shoots, reducing the plant's efficiency. Plants under serious attack can become completely defoliated, the leaves crumbling in the hand. Once an attack is found it is certain all the plants in close proximity will be affected. A hot, dry atmosphere encourages the pest, while moist, humid conditions are inimical to it. Control is first to create the correct environment and spray with derris, dimethoate, bioresmethrin or malathion every five to seven days until cleared. Fumigate or use malathion aerosol; destroy badly infected plants.

□ **THRIPS** (*Heliothrips* ssp. *Thrips tabaci*)

Thrips are small brown or black insects (though often yellow when young) 1–2mm long, slim with four long, narrow wings. Found more outside than inside, this is another insect which thrives upon hot, dry conditions and hates the sprayer. Most damage is caused in the nymph stage, by continual sucking of the sap resulting in silvery white spotting of the foliage which can also take on a pepper and salt effect. Thrips breed rapidly under glass and, if not controlled, breeding goes on continuously, and the higher the temperature the shorter the life cycle. The remedy is to spray with dimethoate, malathion, HCH or to dust with malathion. Fumigate as for aphids.

□ **VINE WEEVIL** (*Otiorrhynchus sulcatus*)

A flightless beetle, brownish black with yellow flecks on wing cases, the vine weevil is easily recognized by its long snout; about 1cm (½in) long with a dull, matt colour rather than shiny. The adult is active in late spring and early summer, eating out notches of the leaves which could easily be attributed to a caterpillar. It is the grub which does untold damage by eating away complete root systems during the winter and early spring. The grub is 1.5cm (⅝in) long, white in colour, crescent shaped with a mahogany brown head; it curls up into a C when unearthed. The beetle lays the eggs in the surface soil near the base of the plant and after hatching the grub starts to feed on the plant's root system.

Grubs are usually found when repotting in the spring, but can be undetected until a plant looks decidedly unhealthy. Upon examination, the whole framework of the plant comes away in the hand with the roots completely eaten away. Control is difficult as both beetle and grubs have to be treated. Late spring and early summer, before egglaying, is the period to eradicate the beetle by fumigating or spraying with HCH or carbaryl. Any suspected grubs can be killed with a thorough watering of a solution of HCH diluted as for spraying. Gamma HCH dust will also be effective if mixed in the compost at the rate of 30g per 5litres, or 4oz to every bushel.

□ **WASPS** (*Vespula vulgaris*)

Fuchsias attacked by wasps result in half-emasculated flowers with sepals and corollas bruised. The workers feed on all sugary substances, seeking the fuchsia flower pollen. Destroying the nests with derris is the only real control as the pest is usually a flying visitor. As with bees, small mesh or netting over ventilators and doors is the other remedy.

□ **WESTERN FLOWER THRIP** (*Frankliniella occidentalis*)

This pest, recently discovered in Britain, was mistaken for the Fuchsia Mite, as it causes similar damage. Difficult to spot with the naked eye, it has a wide host range, including vegetables and flowers. It causes discolouration of the upper leaf surfaces, indentations, speckling, silver deformity, growth malfunc-

(Above) *One of the most beautiful cultivars, 'Seventh Heaven' is a lovely double from California.*

(Opposite) *'Suikerbossie', a recent Dutch introduction, makes a vigorous upright plant and flowers prolifically.*

tions and oedema-like bumps. Adults are tiny slender yellowish insects with narrow wings and are known vectors of some virus diseases. This pest is established in the USA. Control includes using dimethoate or malathion and HCH.

□ WHITE FLY (*Trialeurodes vaporariorum*)

The waxy, white adults, up to 2mm long, fly off in clouds when disturbed, only to find another cover, usually the underside of leaves. At the immobile scale stages they are only just visible. This is another sucking insect which feeds on the sap and excretes honeydew which turns into sooty mould fungus, (*Cladosporium* spp.), closing up the pores of the leaves. This pest is difficult to eradicate, as eggs and scale stages are immune to pesticides; adults must be killed before they breed as there are constant overlapping generations. Spraying or fumigating must be carried out at 5- to 7-day intervals until cleared. The control is frequent sprays of bioresmethrin, diazinon, dimethoate, malathion or resmethrin. Fumigate with HCH or a malathion aerosol.

□ WOODLICE (*Armadillidium nasutum*)

Woodlice have a segmented thorax, grey to yellowish in colour up to 1cm (½in) long, and roll up into ball when disturbed. Omnivorous, they feed upon decaying matter and eat holes in leaves and stems, and will also attack soil and aerial roots. They are always found where rubbish is left lying about and

have two broods a year, of about 50 each time. They favour a warm greenhouse, so control is by good hygiene. Water or dust with HCH, and mixing carbaryl dust into compost will stop root attacks.

DISEASES

□ GREY MOULD (*Botrytis cinerea*)

This is easily identifiable by its grey, hairy fungus and most prevalent in winter and spring. It will affect all types of plants, turning both stems and leaves brown and eventually black. This disease develops only when conditions are wrong: cold, dark, stale and stagnant conditions with no circulation of air coupled with high humidity will encourage this fungal disease. Overcrowding must be avoided and especially during the winter and early spring, a circulation of air moving either by ventilation or heat is essential – the answer is a buoyant atmosphere at all times. Control is effected with benomyl and captan; other fungicides include thiram and sulphur.

□ RUST (*Pucciniastrum epilobii*)

Rust is found on many plants and the fuchsia has its own particular kind. It is readily identified by its reddish brown and orange spore patches on the underside of the leaves, showing as yellow or black spots on the upper surface. It spreads rapidly and can be a very serious disease if not controlled. This disease can easily be 'bought in' or windborne; bees can be responsible. It can be traced to its host plant the willowherb (*Epilobium* spp.). Outbreaks are usually found first inside the greenhouse door or near open roof ventilators; the spread then depends upon the direction of draughts. Rust prevents light from getting to the leaves, restricts the amount of food produced and so stunts growth. Its worst aspect is in being so contagious. Certain control is by hand picking all affected leaves coupled with buoyant atmosphere with good air circulation. Control can also be made with propiconazole and oxycarboxin.

CHAPTER FIVE

TRAINING

Because in its natural habitat, the fuchsia ranges from a creeping, prostrate plant to a tree of great height, we have to grow them artificially, hence the reason for training. The fuchsia is probably the most adaptable of shrubs, so versatile that it can be trained to many recognized forms. This fact does need a little clarification as not every fuchsia will assume all forms. Any fuchsia could be trained as a standard, but the tall, vigorous cultivars are much more suitable candidates, whereas the majority of the introductions from California, with their lax habit, are ideally suited to baskets as trailers, and some are ideal as weeping standards.

First, though, let us look at some guidelines to the general training of all fuchsias.

PRUNING

The fuchsia is a deciduous shrub which needs several months' rest during the winter, unless grown in leaf under the biennial method, after which the remaining growth needs pruning. There are two alternative times for pruning: some growers advocate autumn, whereas the most experienced favour the winter or early spring. With autumn pruning, unless the wood has been ripened, you will be pruning green, sappy growth, resulting in considerable dieback.

Pruning is carried out for several reasons:
(a) to control the size and shape of the plant
(b) to encourage new growth and the formation of new wood
(c) to encourage flowering (fuchsias only flower on new wood)

When is the best time to prune? This is rather difficult to answer by quoting any actual month as it depends upon the conditions prevailing, the amount of heat at your command and the condition of the plants. A loose answer would be that pruning usually takes place during midwinter, late winter or early spring. The correct and short answer is 'just before the sap begins to rise', and the main reason why autumn pruning is not recommended is that the sap can then be high in the stem. A month or six weeks after the shortest day is the time to commence spraying resting plants with clear, tepid water on those suitable days with blue skies and the sun sending

temperatures to around 15–20°C (60–70°F) under glass, but only 1 or 2°C (33–34°F) outside. This spraying softens the old wood and encourages the formation of the new pink eyes or embryo shoots, so helping with an indication of where the new shoots are coming and enabling the shaping of the plants.

Where exactly do we prune? First, cut away all dead and spindly growth, especially anything misplaced. Then adopt the principle of cutting away approximately two-thirds of last year's growth or, to explain in another way, prune back to two or three pairs of eyes on

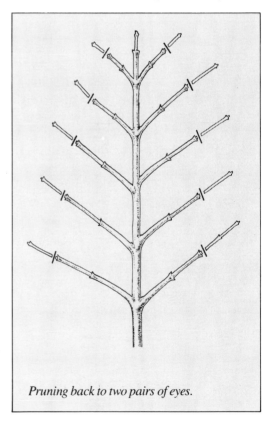

Pruning back to two pairs of eyes.

each lateral. Hard pruning, favoured by show exhibitors, is cutting back to one pair of eyes; medium pruning would be to two pairs and light pruning to three pairs. The last is not favoured as resultant growth would be rather weak and loose. It is unwise to leave pruning too late in the spring when the sap could be high in the stem. Should any cuts be made which ooze sap, make sure the wounds are sealed with a compound to prevent dieback.

The hardy plants outside in the border are not pruned back in the autumn either. These plants should be just shaped back in the autumn by removing one-third of the growth made during summer. The time to prune outside hardies is when the new growth appears at the base of the plant in the early spring and not before. Then prune hard, right back to soil level.

STOPPING

The fuchsia, like a vine, would become unmanageable if left to its own devices and not controlled by pinching or stopping. The object of stopping is to make the plant grow bushier and to

Pruning a hardy fuchsia back to soil level in spring as new growth begins.

obtain shape, very important when growing for exhibition purposes.

To obtain a plant of good shape it is necessary to pinch out the young shoots several times. It is possible to achieve a bush or shrub plant with haphazard stopping, but it is more likely to produce uneven growth. Of course, not all growers require their plants for show purposes, nor do they want to wait until late summer before flowering. The majority want plants for normal decorative use and also for planting out in the border. In such cases just two pinches is adequate: every time a plant is stopped, it delays flowering and it depends upon the type of flower as to how long it is delayed. It is possible to gauge when a plant will be in full flower by estimating the period between the last stopping and full flowering potential. Experience has shown the period to be 60 days for single flowers, 70 days for semi-doubles and 80 days for double flowers to be in full bloom from the last stopping. However, all cultivars are not the same; temperature and other weather conditions can delay or hasten flowers, consequently the times quoted must be regarded as approximate. Some cultivars, such as 'Snowcap', 'Display', 'Bon Accorde', 'Rufus' and 'Tennessee Waltz' are early flowerers, while 'Mission Bells', 'Leonora', 'Countess of Aberdeen' and 'Flirtation Waltz' are renowned as late flowering.

It is well at this juncture to mention that when plants are planted out in the border, no further stopping is made after the initial stopping made in the early cultivation. It is a phenomenon of nature that once a plant is established outside in the border, it becomes self-branching and without any further aid, produces a perfectly symmetrical bush.

Leaves of the fuchsia grow in a cruciform manner, one pair of leaves growing one way while the next pair grow in the opposite direction. After any stopping the embryo shoots left in the leaf axil will produce shoots pointing in the same direction as the leaf in whose axil the embryo shoots lie. To decide, therefore, in which direction you wish the new shoots to develop, observe where the new pairs of leaves are forming in the axil, pointing in the direction of your required line of growth. You can now stop at one, two or three pairs of leaves. If you stop after either one or three pairs of leaves, the plant will branch out in growth at right angles. Should you stop after two pairs of leaves, the plant will branch out in the same direction as the original growth.

The timing of any stopping is important; too early pinching can result in the removal of the small buds or embryo shoots, together with the pair of small leaves. On the other hand, pinching out too late will result in checking the growth. Not until the shoot you are stopping has made sufficient growth, approximately 6 or 8 mm ($\frac{1}{4}$–$\frac{1}{3}$ in), should it be removed, making sure you do not damage or remove those tender new buds. The best implement is the finger and thumb – if you cannot get your finger and thumb in, then the shoot is not yet large enough to remove. Another implement could be fine

Still the best red and white, 'Swingtime' remains a top favourite on everybody's list.

pointed scissors for very small growth, but these have the tendency to crush the fine tissue. The final point to bear in mind is that once you start to stop a plant, all the shoots must be stopped at the same time, otherwise erratic flowering will result.

TRAINING OF BUSH FUCHSIAS

This is the easiest shape to train and, together with the standard, the most suitable for landscaping and outdoor cultivation. It is however, a recognized shape and not something that just happens; it is a plant grown either on a single stem or on shoots produced at or below soil level. The former would be classified as a bush plant, the latter as a shrub type.

The best bushes or shrubs are formed from a fairly vigorous cultivar, not lax or trailing, raised as an early spring cutting or struck in the autumn. The time to start training, and this applies not only to bush or shrub training but to all types of training, is when the cutting has made both good root and top growth. This is when the rooted cutting is in its first or second pot, either 6cm (2¼in) or 8cm (3in).

When the plant has developed three pairs of leaves, remove the centre growing tip, this will be the first stop or pinch. This action encourages side shoots to develop in the axils of the leaves. When these have made two pairs of leaves, these are also stopped. This now means that instead of just one central shoot, we have increased to six

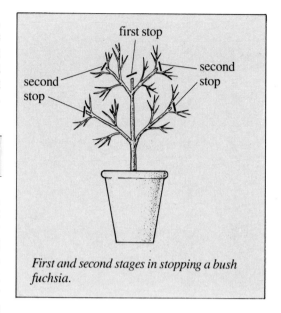

First and second stages in stopping a bush fuchsia.

shoots. From these resultant six shoots all will break again and the tips are pinched at a further two pairs of leaves; this is our third stop, and there are now not six but 24 shoots. For normal decorative use this is sufficient, but should large specimen plants be required then this stopping procedure can be continued until the required size and shape has been achieved. It is well to remember that each stopping delays flowering by approximately two months. It is important that all shoots are stopped at the same time, otherwise part of the plant will be in flower and the other parts either in leaf or small bud stage.

While stopping and training is taking place, it is essential to keep the plant growing steadily by repeated moves into new pots; from 8cm (3in) to 10cm (4in) and when the roots are working nicely around the sides of the pot, from 10 cm (4 in) to 13 cm (5 in). On current growth, that is, a first-year plant, a 13 cm (5 in) pot will be sufficient, but with very vigorous cultivars, it is possible to move finally into a 15 cm (6 in) pot. At each stage of potting on plants should be protected from excessive sunlight for two or three days to overcome the check; newly potted plants placed in direct sunlight will wilt and receive a severe setback. After watering with a fine-rosed can, place in the shadiest part of the greenhouse, which could be under the staging.

Another aspect of cultivation around this time is the turning routine. Every plant on the staging or elsewhere needs to be turned a half-turn every third day; this will prevent plants growing more on one 'side' than another.

TRAINING OF STANDARD FUCHSIAS

Standards are usually the next type of training attempted by enthusiasts. These are, in fact, bush or shrub plants growing on a stem of a desired length. Standards are eminently suitable for all types of bedding schemes and landscaping where height is required, particularly as 'dot' plants.

Standards fall into certain categories and are classified by the length of clear stem from soil level to the lowest branch or lateral. It is not necessary to adhere to the following measurements defined by the British Fuchsia Society, but they are definitions by which balance and proportion can be attained:

> 152 mm (6 in) – 254 mm (10 in) for mini-standards
> 254 mm (10 in) – 457 mm (18 in) for quarter-standards
> 457 mm (18 in) – 762 mm (30 in) for half-standards
> 762 mm (30 in) – 1067 mm (42 in) for full-standards

Select the early, spring-rooted cutting of a strong, upright and vigorous cultivar such as 'Snowcap' or, if deciding upon a weeping standard, a cultivar with a lax or trailing habit such as 'Marinka'. Some cultivars such as 'Barbara' or Snowcap' often throw three leaves in the leaf axil instead of the normal two; in selecting this type even better specimen plants will be produced. The rooted cutting is grown on without stopping from its initial 6 cm (2¼) pot, then when the 8 cm (3 in) pot stage has been reached, sufficient growth will have been made to need early support. This is important as when 10 or 15 cm (4 or 6 in) of stem has been made, a cane is inserted and tied, not too loosely, at intervals of 5 cm (2 in) throughout the period of training. Although a tedious operation, it will ensure a good straight stem, the hallmark of any good standard. While height and rapid growth are being achieved by means of a high nitrogenous fertilizer, the turning procedure will ensure even growth.

The next stage is also important. While this growth takes place, all the side shoots appearing in the leaf axil are removed, but not the leaves – these are retained for breathing and feeding. The leaves are not removed until the

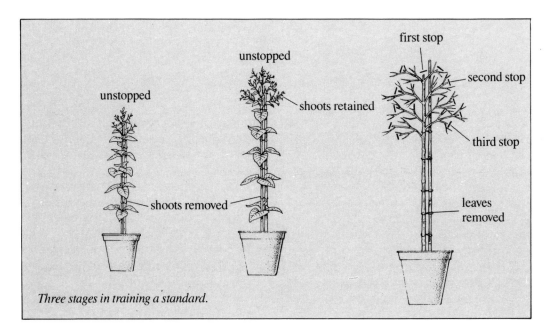

Three stages in training a standard.

intended height and ultimate top head has been achieved. When removing the side shoots, you must always leave the uppermost three pairs of shoots on the stem. The object from now on is to obtain rapid and unchecked growth, achieved by constant potting on, increasing the pot size just 2–2½cm (1 in) at a time.

Constant attention must be paid to the condition of the root system. As soon as they have worked themselves around the outside, the plant must be potted on. Should the young whip, as it is now called, become pot bound, it will tend to bud and flower; in no circumstance must this be allowed to happen while it is still attaining the desired height. Should bud or flower develop, upright growth will be retarded and even if removed will act as a stop. The

ultimate pot sizes would be 14cm (5¼in) for the mini-standard, 15cm (6in) for the quarter, 18cm (7in) for the half-standard and 20cm (8in) or even larger for the full standard. When potting on, increase the length of cane to some 15–30cm (6–12in) above the plant's actual height.

Feeding should not be overlooked; nitrogenous fertilizer right up to bud stage will assist in the desired rapid growth.

Just before the desired height has been made, make certain of having at least 3 pairs of shoots at the top. When sufficent height has been achieved, grow on until four pairs of shoots are present; these must be retained to develop into the head. Now is the time to make the definitive stop by removing the leader or uppermost terminal shoot. The ideal

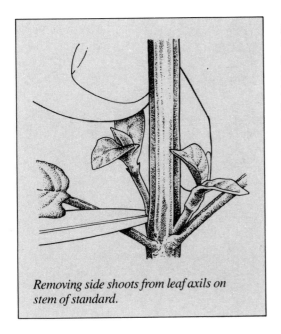

Removing side shoots from leaf axils on stem of standard.

number of side shoots left at the top would be four pairs; leave more if desired to form an even larger head, these are now left to grow on exactly the same as on a bush plant, being pinched out at each two pairs of leaves; usually three stops are all that is necessary to form a well-developed head. For a very 'tight' head you would pinch out at each pair of leaves, after the initial stopping of two pairs.

When the finished standard has been achieved, all the leaves are stripped off below the head, which produces the bare stem. To obtain balance, the finished head should be approximately one-third of the total height and the width about two-thirds of the total height. If by chance the ultimate standard has not been made by late autumn, it will be necessary to keep the plant in

green leaf throughout the winter for completion the following spring. When growing mini-standards, which can easily be flowered in the same season, they must be of balanced proportions and the selection of suitable cultivars is of paramount importance. Concentrate upon the smaller flowering cultivars and even with these singles to be preferred to doubles.

When considering winter care for established standards, it is necessary to maintain 4°C (40°F) for resting purposes, as all tall plants are more susceptible to frost and lower temperatures, and the sap must be retained in the head and not allowed to dry out.

IN BASKETS

Baskets viewed from eye level are unquestionably both spectacular and eye-catching. While they take up much space in the greenhouse, they are ideal subjects for outside work and can be utilized to great effect in conjunction with pergolas. The basic principle to obtain good baskets is that growth should fill the centre and top and continue to surge over the edges in a sweeping cascade. The growth should be uniform, with clean foliage and an abundance of flower, which should obscure the basket.

The ideal time of planting is early to mid-spring – an early start is required to produce the long, trailing laterals. My experience has proved that baskets are far superior grown on current growth, discarding old baskets and starting each spring with new plants; if you can obtain

A 35 cm (14 in) basket planted with five plants of one variety in spring.

baskets 1.5 m (5 ft) across why bother with old plants?

Baskets can be of various sizes, both full and half baskets and in a variety of materials. Those in galvanized wire are to be preferred, although plastic-covered wire now seems to be almost universal. Sizes can range between 25 cm (10 in) and 38 cm (15 in) while the half baskets are usually either 30 cm (12 in) or 35 cm (14 in), measured across the back.

When planting it is more correct to plant just one type of cultivar per basket. In this way, growth, balance and flowering are all more easily controlled and maintained. The number of plants to a basket is recommended as three young plants (from 9 cm [3½ in] pots) to the 25 cm (10 in) basket, four plants to the 30 cm (12 in) and five plants for the 35 cm (14 in) or 38 cm (15 cm) basket. Suitable cultivars are plentiful but they must be of the trailing or lax habit; upright cultivars are totally unsuitable.

Select plants grown from early spring cuttings grown on into 9 cm (3½ in) pots. If not available from your own stock, order well in advance and obtain from a specialist fuchsia nurseryman. These plants should be stopped after two or three pairs of leaves before planting. From then on the pinching procedure is easy to remember: pinch out at every three pairs of leaves. This may not always be possible; if not, revert to every two pairs. Carry on pinching as quickly as growth allows and aim to get at least three pinches – four will be even better. The fourth will need time and much patience as pinches will be in excess of one hundred.

The actual planting should not take place on the kitchen table: baskets have, or should have, rounded bottoms and are impossible to balance. It is better to place the basket in a very large flower pot or a bucket, to obtain stability and control. Line the basket with green moss, if obtainable; if not resort to either a peat liner or sheet of polythene. Make sure when using the two latter that sufficient small holes are made in the base to ensure essential drainage. When the basket is lined, place a fair quantity of sphagnum peat on the bottom, then nearly fill the basket with a good soilless compost. A soil-based compost might result in a superior basket, but the weight of the basket will be excessive. Each plant should be set not vertically, but planted around the edge of the basket at an angle of 45 degrees. When completed the plants will already be in a slightly trailing position leaving a space in the middle. Plant one small plant if you so wish, but it is not necessary as the spread of growth will quickly cover the entire top. Firm in each plant with finger pressure, leaving the top with a saucer-shaped depression for watering purposes. Water in well with the fine-rosed can, place the basket in a shady position for a few days, before bringing out to its final position. Keep fairly dry immediately after watering, almost to the point of drying out, and try not to let the overhanging laterals rest upon the wire of the basket – there is a tendency for damping off to take place if contact is made early in growth.

When placing outside, whether in a landscaping scheme or hanging from a pergola, a wall or under trees, make sure they go outside before they bud – baskets never flower well if placed out while in bloom.

There are many other forms of training which are spectacular but rather complicated and time-consuming. Cordons, espaliers, pillars and pyramids are not really suitable for landscaping, are rarely seen these days and so are not included in this book. It is possible, however, to use 'portable gardens' (pp. 25–26) to create similar effects.

CHAPTER SIX

PROPAGATION

The fuchsia is one of the easiest of plants to cultivate and also the easiest of plants to propagate. There are several ways of propagating, orthodox and unorthodox; however, most enthusiasts are interested in the approved manner and my intention is to explain those methods which I have carried out personally with success.

With fuchsias there are three recognized methods by which they can be reproduced: grafting, seed or cuttings. Another method of obtaining new cultivars other than by seed is by mutating or sporting, but this is not strictly a method of propagation.

Grafting is very rarely used except when a slow-growing cultivar or a weak grower is required as a standard. As the operation takes almost 18 months to complete, carried out in a close atmosphere on well-ripened wood, anything achieved by grafting can be accomplished quicker and more easily by cuttings. Propagating by seed is the method by which new cultivars are raised, whereas if we require an exact replica of an existing fuchsia, then we resort to the taking of cuttings.

RAISING PLANTS FROM CUTTINGS

Almost all the fuchsia plants grown are raised from cuttings and it is the only method by which we can obtain a plant exactly the same as the original. Provided the right conditions exist and cuttings are available, they can be struck at any time of the year and no grower should be satisfied with less than 95% strike. Obviously there are periods of the year when better results can be obtained, but the real success lies in the type of cutting rather than the method, the medium used, whether hormone powders are used or the kind of plant ultimately produced.

The ideal time for striking is early spring and the ideal type of cutting is the tip cutting. There are, however, three types of cuttings: the normal cutting with three or four pairs of leaves, 8–10 cm (3–4 in) long; the intermediate with two or three pairs of leaves; and the little tip cutting, which describes itself. The first requirement is a cutting

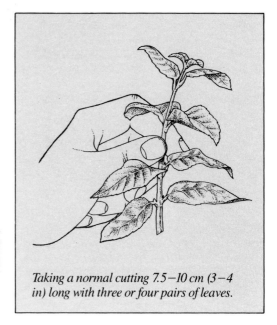

Taking a normal cutting 7.5–10 cm (3–4 in) long with three or four pairs of leaves.

with leaflets growing actively from the tip. Cuttings should be taken only from healthy plants and should not carry either buds or flowers – the cutting cannot develop flowers and root at the same time. This does not mean that you cannot take a cutting carrying bud or flower – you can, but bud and flower must be removed and the resultant cutting is somewhat inferior to a non-flowering cutting. Look for cuttings possessing three leaves instead of the normal two at each axil. 'Snowcap', 'Checkerboard', 'Barbara' and 'Mephisto' are typical examples, as are many of Lye's cultivars, which are especially suitable for growing on as standards. Cuttings should be taken as soft as possible; the harder the cutting the longer and more difficult it is to strike. Soft wooded cuttings are also more reliable and taken during late winter to mid-spring.

Most specialized nurserymen start their main batches as soon as the day turns longer, in midwinter, with the help of artificial lighting (preferably fluorescent containing a high percentage of red colouring), temperatures approaching 13°C (55°F) and with the aid of mist and soil-warming cables giving a bottom heat of around 18°C (65°F). We amateurs do not have all these advantages, but nevertheless have to make sure that our tender young cuttings never lack moisture and warmth, but above all we must prevent them from wilting.

☐ STANDARD AND INTERMEDIATE CUTTINGS

When taking an 8–10cm (3–4in) cutting, trim off the bottom pairs of leaves, leaving one or two pairs of leaves together with the tip bud; in the case of the intermediate cutting, remove just the bottom pair of leaves. Cut cleanly just below the node or leaf joint with a very sharp knife or razor blade. The cut must be clean and the cutting not left with any length of stem or snag, which has a tendency to rot, with subsequent loss of the cutting. The object of cutting just below the leaf joint is so that the concentration of natural rooting hormones in the joint will then be at the base of the cutting. You can use a rooting hormone powder if so inclined, but fuchsia cuttings strike so readily on account of the hormone activity at the base, that they are not really necessary. Hormone preparations will never trans-

form a weak or clumsy cutting into a good one; they can, however, hasten rooting and assist only if every other condition is favourable.

Guard against damping off or botrytis by bathing cuttings in a solution of a fungicide, totally immersing for a few seconds before insertion in rooting medium. The medium in which cuttings are struck is not critical – many growers still favour the old combination of equal parts of peat and sand, but the peat should be sphagnum and not sedge peat, whereas the sand should be washed and not builders' sand or sea sand. Some prefer soilless composts, others use pure sand or all peat, perlite or vermiculite can be used. Cuttings can be easily struck in water, but this has a serious disadvantage, in that the roots produced are extremely brittle and easily broken off when potting off. At the British Fuchsia Society demonstration tables in recent years, one medium in which cuttings were struck was nothing else but toilet paper, with no particular preference to colour! My favourite striking medium, used with great success, is 80% Humber soilless compost with 20% perlite. It will be observed that all the composts quoted have one thing in common – they contain no or very little feed or fertilizer. After a few days in the medium the base of the cutting forms a callus over the wound where it was severed from the mother plant. The cutting immediately starts to demand both food and moisture, which results in the callused base sending out feelers in search of nourishment and moisture to counteract transpiration. Now if there

A magnificent plant of 'Thalia', the best of the triphylla cultivars, raised in Germany.

exists a supply of food in the striking medium, the young feelers or undeveloped roots become lazy, but without food they are forced to search further and thus the root system is formed.

The actual container in which cuttings are struck is immaterial as long as it is shallow. It could be a seed tray, half pots, peat pots, Jiffy 7s, a segmented tray in thin plastic; my favourite container is the white polystyrene bottomless tray with 48 divisions.

The next advice is all important. Never push cuttings into the medium; this practice is both lazy and likely to damage the tender stem of the cutting and prevent rooting. Having made a hole in the medium with a dibber or blunt piece of wood, insert your cutting about 2–2.5 cm (¾–1 in) into the rooting medium, taking care to space the cuttings to avoid the leaves touching – overlapping leaves tend to adhere to each other and cause damping off. It is essential that the cuttings are inserted firmly, with no air pockets; they should resist a very slight tug of the fingers, using both dibber and fingers. Water in well with a fine-rosed can which settles in the cuttings and prevents caking of the surface; overwatering after this initial watering is a common cause of failure to root.

Semi-double 'Westminster Chimes' is ideal for a hanging pot.

Once a shoot is detached, it immediately loses its supply of moisture, but it will still lose moisture through its leaves, which cannot now be replaced naturally. This transpiration must be halted if the cutting is not to. become dehydrated and wilt. To overcome this, after placing in a close atmosphere, cuttings will need to be sprayed with clear water. This could be once or twice during the day, according to the weather conditions and the heat provided. The close atmosphere is provided by means of a propagating frame or enclosure, preferably with bottom heat. The term heat does not imply a high temperature, simply gentle warmth needed around the severed stems of the cuttings, where the production of roots is to be encouraged. Bottom heat is usually provided by means of electric soil-warming cables in a bed of sand and capable of maintaining a temperature between 13 and 18°C (55–65°F), but is really subject to the grower's ingenuity. The type of propagator used need not be expensive, any home-made enclosure of simple design using polythene can be used, a bottomless box with a sheet of glass on top, or standard seed trays and pots can be utilized with a range of plastic dome covers. If no propagator is available, insert a small pot of your cuttings into a polythene bag, tie near the top to form a tent, keeping the polythene clear of the leaves with a couple of sticks, and place in a warm but shaded position. This would need little attention and after four weeks will produce rooted cuttings. Cuttings in the propagating frames will, apart from the necessary spraying and turning of the glass, have to be shaded from any strong direct sunlight. This is essential to prevent the young, tender cuttings from dying, either from 'cooking' under extreme heat, or from wilting. Once cuttings have wilted it is extremely unlikely that they will recover.

Soft wooded cuttings will root in 10 to 14 days under ideal conditions. As soon as the cuttings have rooted, a slight change takes place in the colour, they look a little darker green with a lighter centre, and look decidedly cheeky, upright and proud. Rooted cuttings

will quite definitely resist that little tug from the fingers. At this stage or even a little earlier, ventilation can be introduced and increased gradually until the cuttings remain upright with covers removed. Then, rather than heavy overhead watering, continue with overhead spraying and shading from direct, strong sunlight. As soon as the cuttings have established a good root system, I have found that by spacing out into standard seed trays with only 12 to a tray, far superior root systems are produced with a free root run, rather than potting off into conventional 5 cm (2 in) pots. This method saves a potting-on stage as the plants can be moved into 8 cm (3 in) pots direct from the seed trays and so make superior plants.

☐ TIP CUTTINGS
The other soft wooded cutting, which is far superior and my own preference, is

Well-rooted cutting ready to be potted off.

the tip cutting. This produces a much stronger and shorter root system, a stronger plant much more easily trained, especially for shrub training and 9 cm (3½ in) pot work, as shoots are

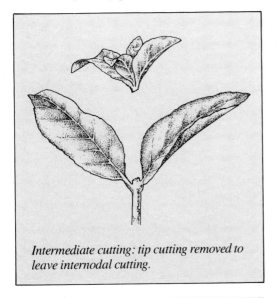

Intermediate cutting: tip cutting removed to leave internodal cutting.

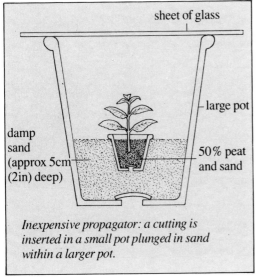

sheet of glass

large pot

damp sand (approx 5cm (2in) deep)

50% peat and sand

Inexpensive propagator: a cutting is inserted in a small pot plunged in sand within a larger pot.

often produced at soil level and below.

This cutting describes itself, being just the tip with a pair of leaves. These are soft and tender and must be handled very carefully, as the lower leaves cannot be removed in this instance for obvious reasons. The sharp, clean cut just below the leaf joint is still made, but with little or no stem, the cutting cannot be placed into a proper hole, so a depression on the surface of the medium is made and the cutting firmly pressed in with dibber and fingers. All other points are the same as for normal and intermediate cuttings.

The tip cutting is very suitable for both the easiest and cheapest type of propagator, the discarded coffee jar. Four little tip cuttings can be struck around the edge of a 5.5 cm (2¼ in) pot, which will just pass through the neck of the coffee jar. After the initial watering in, the lid is screwed up tight making the jar airtight, placed in a shady part of the greenhouse or kitchen window sill and left for several weeks. The only attention while rooting takes place, is the occasional opening to release any excessive condensation and moisture. The cuttings are not watered at any time during rooting, which normally takes three to four weeks, after which air is applied and the little plants can subsequently be potted off. Cuttings can be taken in mid autumn, but these have to be maintained during the whole winter in green leaf, which means a temperature of 7°C (45°F). Cuttings in coffee jars are very suitable, as autumn cuttings are usually potted off in late winter.

APPENDIX

FUCHSIA SOCIETIES

After unparalleled enthusiasm for fuchsias in the Victorian era, interest waned considerably during the early years of this century. But between the two World Wars two societies which were to become famous were formed: the American Fuchsia Society in 1929, and the British Fuchsia Society, under the title of the Fuchsia Society, in 1938.

The society in Britain was founded with the object of furthering interest in the cultivation of the fuchsia, and its successful launching was due to the efforts of W. W. Whiteman of Gloucester, who during the difficult war years served as Secretary and Treasurer, ably supported by Lady Boothby, the Society's first President. The third member, the Revd. H. Bertie Brown who died only recently in 1988, acted as society consultant.

When first formed, the Fuchsia Society gave the impression of an exclusive club, boasting a membership of just under 200, with nearly all of its officers possessing titles or being people of renown or influence.

The society struggled to promote the fuchsia to its former glory, and interest gradually grew. Soon after 1945 the Fuchsia Society changed its name to the British Fuchsia Society. In America, mainly in California, new cultivars were imported and both hybridization and interest reached new heights. By 1955 the membership of the British Fuchsia Society had risen to 537, with a bank balance of £216 and with well-known names including William Punker Wood, author of *Fuchsia Survey* (the first recognized British book on fuchsias, still an authoritative work today), who became its President in 1949.

Around this period other famous names such as Sir Ralph Newman, Charles Unwin, Bernard Rawlins and Margaret Slater, current BFS Chairman, appeared within the Society. Wilfred Sharp, of impeccable stature as honorary secretary and treasurer, together with the renowned hybridizers and outstanding personalities James Travis and Thomas Thorne, were generating keen interest and by 1958 the membership reached the 1000 mark for the first time.

August 1957 saw the first National Show outside London being held at Sale, Manchester, under the organization of Harry Leytham who was to carry out this office for the next 18 years.

By the time Stanley Wilson held office in 1961 the membership had quadrupled itself to 2050. Interest in the fuchsia was now increasing all over the country and while the British Fuchsia Society was performing yeoman service, it was considered by many enthusiasts to be rather remote. This was the trigger, set off by Stanley Cash, for the commencement of local societies being formed up and down the country. The Dorking Society, founded by Dorothea Flower, was the first to form, in January 1964, closely followed by Leicestershire in February of the next year. The next society to form was in London at Barnet in September 1966, followed in the next year by Harrow, Thames Valley based at Hounslow and Edenbridge in Kent. Another London society at Enfield formed their society just two days before the Northampton Society on October 17, 1967.

The name of the author first appears as holding office within the BFS in 1966, the same year Stanley Wilson held office as President. From that year until 1972, the BFS possessed their finest editor in Stanley Cash, whose publications are still unsurpassed. The exceptionally fine hybridists George Roe (1970) and Clifford Gadsby (1972) both held some office, while the present secretary and treasurer Ron Ewart, first appeared on the fuchsia scene in 1973.

It was in 1972 that the first Whiteman Medal of Honour was awarded to James Travis, followed by Margaret Slater in 1975, for services not only to the Society but to the fuchsia in general. Clifford Gadsby received the same award posthumously a few years later, to be followed in 1980 by Wilfred Sharp and afterwards to Stanley Cash, George Roe and the Revd H. Bertie Brown. The most recent award of this Medal was made to the author in 1986. Since 1975 and up to the present day Norman Hobbs, George Bartlett, Edwin Goulding and Reginald Witts have all held office and rendered valuable service.

The present membership of the British Fuchsia Society is at the almost record number of 6000, with as many as 300 affiliated societies and is the second largest specialist society in the country. Membership allows free admission and free entries on the showbench at shows organized by the Society. Members are entitled to the *Fuchsia Annual* and Bulletins in addition to free advice on all matters concerning fuchsia culture. National Shows are currently held during the summer months at London, Manchester (Sale), Birmingham or Nottingham, Worthing, Chippenham, Harrogate, Central Scotland, Wales and East Anglia. The current Honorary Secretary is: R. Ewart, 29 Princess Crescent, Dollar, Clackmannanshire. Local societies, most of which are affiliated to the BFS, hold their independent shows and are established in all parts of Britain. All hold regular meetings, with talks and lectures and their shows are judged in accordance with BFS standards. Details of the nearest society are available from the BFS Secretary or from the author.

With the worldwide interest ever increasing it is not surprising to find national societies formed all over the world. Shows in Britain are largely competitive, but elsewhere the emphasis is on exhibiting. America possesses two national bodies, each based in California. The American Fuchsia Society centred at San Francisco was established in 1929 and today has a membership of approximately 1500. It is an organization that encourages fuchsia culture all over the world, grants scholarships and among other activities fosters scientific research. In addition the Society is the International Authority for the Registration and Nomenclature of the Fuchsia. Their monthly Bulletin serves as a clearing house for articles on culture and includes a colour cover, illustrating a different fuchsia every issue. Membership is automatically available to those who join one of its branches which include, Coos Bay – Fort Bragg – Fort Dick – Eureka – Healdsburg – Jose – Los Altos – Novato Pacifica – Petaluma – Pinole-Rohnert Park – Sacramento – Salem – San Bruno – San Francisco – San Mateo – San Rafael – San Rosa – Sebastopol – Vallejo and Yamhill. Information is available from the American Fuchsia Society, Hall of Flowers, 9th Avenue and Lincoln Way, San Francisco, California.

The other American Society is the National Fuchsia Society with a membership of around 1000 based in Southern California, with branches centred upon Costa Mesa – Downey – Garden Grove – Glendale – Long Beach – Oceanside – Palos Verdes – Redondo – San Diego – Renton Wa – Ventura and Whitter. This society also publishes a monthly 'Fuchsia Fan' with front col-

oured cover. Contact can be made at the National Fuchsia Society 2892 Crown View Drive, Rancho, Palos Verdes, California.

The enthusiasm in the North West of USA is based around the areas of Seattle and Puget Sound, Washington known as the Northwest Fuchsia Society. Formed in 1983, it has seven affiliated societies with a total membership of approximately 850. Contact address is P.O. Box 33785, Bitter Lake Station, Seattle, Washington 98133.

The interest in Canada is centred in Vancouver with the formation of the British Columbia Fuchsia Society in 1961. Their membership is around the 300 figure with regular publications and having recently celebrated their 25th anniversary. The current Correspondence Secretary is Lorna Herchenson, 2402 Swinburne Avenue, North Vancouver, B.C., V7H 1L2.

Another much smaller society, the Greater Victoria Fuchsia Society, was formed in 1979 and is based at Victoria B.C. The mailing address is P.O. Box 5266, Postal Station B, Victoria B.C. The Dutch National Society is the second largest national society, with between 2000 and 3000 members. Other national societies are to be found in Australia, Austria, Belgium, Canada, Denmark, France, New Zealand, Norway, South Africa, Sweden, Switzerland, West Germany and Zimbabwe. The author will gladly furnish details of suitable contacts on application.

Containers can sometimes be stacked to create an 'instant pillar'. This pillar is planted with the varieties 'Marinka' and 'Snowcap'.

INDEX

ACKNOWLEDGEMENTS

The publishers are grateful to the author, Leo B. Boullemier, for granting permission to reproduce all the colour photographs for this book, with the exception of those on pp. 8, 37 and 40, which were taken by Bob Challinor. Acknowledgement is also made to the unknown copyright holder of the print, which appears on p. 16.
All the line drawings are by Nils Solberg.
The publishers are also grateful to the British Fuchsia Society for granting permission to reproduce the quotation on p. 31, which was written by Thom Thorne.